# LEARN TO
# Crochet for Baby

Sweet Posies, page 79

## www.companyscoming.com
### visit our website

Fancy Footwear, page 98

# Learn to Crochet for Baby

Copyright © Company's Coming Publishing Limited

All rights reserved worldwide. No part of this book may be reproduced, stored in a retrieval system or transmitted in any form by any means without permission in advance from the publisher.

In the case of photocopying or other reprographic copying, a license may be purchased from the Canadian Copyright Licensing Agency (Access Copyright). Visit www.accesscopyright.ca or call 1-800-893-5777. In the United States, please contact the Copyright Clearance Centre, www.copyright.com or call 978-750-8400.

Brief portions of this book may be reproduced for review purposes, provided credit is given to the source. Reviewers are invited to contact the publisher for additional information.

The contents of this publication were provided especially for Company's Coming Publishing Limited under an exclusive license agreement with the copyright owner, DRG Texas, LP ("DRG"). The contents are not available for commercial use or sale outside of this publication, but are intended only for personal use. Every effort has been made to ensure that the instructions in this publication are complete and accurate; however, neither DRG nor Company's Coming Publishing Limited can be held responsible for any human error, typographical mistake or variation in the results achieved by the user.

First Printing April 2011

**Library and Archives Canada Cataloguing in Publication**
Learn to crochet for baby.
(Workshop series)
Includes index.
ISBN 978-1-897477-49-6
1. Crocheting--Patterns. 2. Infants' clothing. 3. Blankets. 4. Crocheting.
I. Title: Crochet for baby. II. Series: Workshop series (Edmonton, Alta.)
TT820.L423 2011        746.43'40432        C2010-903665-4

Published by
**Company's Coming Publishing Limited**
2311-96 Street
Edmonton, Alberta, Canada T6N 1G3
Tel: 780-450-6223  Fax: 780-450-1857
www.companyscoming.com

Printed in China

# The Company's Coming Story

Jean Paré grew up with an understanding that family, friends and home cooking are the key ingredients for a good life. A mother of four, Jean worked as a professional caterer for 18 years, operating out of her home kitchen. During that time, she came to appreciate quick and easy recipes that call for everyday ingredients. In answer to mounting requests for her recipes, Company's Coming cookbooks were born, and Jean moved on to a new chapter in her career.

In the beginning, Jean worked from a spare bedroom in her home, located in the small prairie town of Vermilion, Alberta, Canada. The first Company's Coming cookbook, *150 Delicious Squares*, was an immediate bestseller. Today, with well over 150 titles in print, Company's Coming has earned the distinction of publishing Canada's most popular cookbooks. The company continues to gain new supporters by adhering to Jean's "Golden Rule of Cooking"—Never share a recipe you wouldn't use yourself. It's an approach that has worked—millions of times over!

Company's Coming cookbooks are distributed throughout Canada, the United States, Australia and other international English-language markets. French and Spanish language editions have also been published. Sales to date have surpassed 25 million copies with no end in sight. Familiar and trusted in home kitchens around the world, Company's Coming cookbooks are highly regarded both as kitchen workbooks and as family heirlooms.

Company's Coming founder Jean Paré

Just as Company's Coming continues to promote the tradition of home cooking, the same is now true with crafting. Like good cooking, great craft results depend upon easy-to-follow instructions, readily available materials and enticing photographs of the finished products. Also like cooking, crafting is meant to be enjoyed in the home or cottage. Company's Coming Crafts, then, is a natural extension from the kitchen into the family room or den.

Because Company's Coming operates a test kitchen and not a craft shop, we've partnered with a major North American craft content publisher to assemble a variety of craft compilations exclusively for us. Our editors have been involved every step of the way. You can see the excellent results for yourself in the book you're holding.

Company's Coming Crafts are for everyone—whether you're a beginner or a seasoned pro. What better gift could you offer than something you've made yourself? In these hectic days, people still enjoy crafting parties; they bring family and friends together in the same way a good meal does. Company's Coming is proud to support crafters with this new creative book series.

We hope you enjoy these easy-to-follow, informative and colourful books, and that they inspire your creativity. So, don't delay—get crafty!

# TABLE OF CONTENTS

## Sugar & Spice

*Create a wardrobe for your little girl that will be the talk of the town.*

## Bouncing Baby Boy

*Dress your little man in style with these cute crocheted designs.*

Beach Baby Ensemble, 36

Pretty in Pink Sweater, page 43

Sunday Pink,
page 20

Baby Letter Jacket, page 68

# TABLE OF CONTENTS

## Cuddle-Up Baby Blankets

*Little ones will be snug and cozy in these hand-stitched blankets.*

## Heads & Toes

*Hats and booties make the perfect gift for your precious little ones.*

Teddy Bear Set, page 118

Soft as a Cloud, page 82

Grandma's Double Delight, page 88

Ruffles & Roses, page 110

# Make it yourself!

## CRAFT WORKSHOP SERIES

Get a craft class in a book! General instructions teach basic skills or how to apply them in a new way. Easy-to-follow steps, diagrams and photos make projects simple.

Whether paper crafting, knitting, crocheting, beading, sewing or quilting—find beautiful, fun designs you can make yourself.

*For a complete listing of Company's Coming cookbooks and craft books, check out*
## www.companyscoming.com

# FOREWORD

Babies are bundles of joy and the perfect excuse for keeping our crochet hooks in motion. Everyone wants to make something special for a new baby, and a handmade gift is just about the nicest thing you can give to a loved one or friend. Whether you are crocheting for your own child, grandchild, great-grandchild or friend, you will find unique designs in *Learn to Crochet for Baby* that will express your love and, at the same time, create heirloom treasures for years to come.

And while you have your hooks out, it's a good time to remember those going through traumatic times with their little ones. During times such as these, it means a lot to the family just knowing that someone thinks enough of their child to take the time out of their busy day for someone they may never know. Donations of hats, blankets and booties are quick-to-stitch and much appreciated by your local children's hospital or women's shelter, and such a comfort for a baby born premature or with disabilities.

In *Learn to Crochet for Baby*, you'll find 37 beautiful designs ranging from quick-to-stitch to more intricate projects. The Sugar & Spice chapter is filled with sweet little dresses, sweaters and even a teeny-weeny bikini complete with a cover-up. Your little one will be the centre of attention when he wears the Baby Letter Jacket, or the cute-as-pie Little Boy Blue sweater and hat found in the Bouncing Baby Boy chapter. The Cuddle-Up Baby Blankets chapter will delight you with blankets of all shapes, sizes and colours, with project skill levels ranging from easy to intermediate. The adorable hats, socks and shoes found in the Heads & Toes chapter make the perfect take-along project to work on.

We hope you have as much fun stitching these projects as we did putting this book together for you.

Receiving Blanket & Booties, page 95

# CROCHET BASICS

## Reading Patterns

Crochet patterns are written in a special language full of abbreviations, asterisks, parentheses, brackets and other symbols and terms. These short forms are used so instructions will not take up too much space. They may seem confusing at first, but once understood, they are easy to follow.

## Abbreviations

**beg** begin/begins/beginning

**bpdc** back post double crochet

**bpsc** back post single crochet

**bptr** back post treble crochet

**CC** contrasting colour

**ch(s)** chain stitch(es)

**ch–** refers to chain or space previously made (i.e. ch-1 space)

**ch sp(s)** chain space(s)

**cl(s)** cluster(s)

**cm** centimetre(s)

**dc** double crochet (singular/plural)

**dc dec** double crochet 2 or more stitches together, as indicated

**dec** decrease/decreases/decreasing

**dtr** double treble crochet

**ext** extended

**fpdc** front post double crochet

**fpsc** front post single crochet

**fptr** front post treble crochet

**g** gram(s)

**hdc** half double crochet

**hdc dec** half double crochet 2 or more stitches together, as indicated

**inc** increase/increases/increasing

**lp(s)** loops(s)

**MC** main colour

**mm** millimetre(s)

**oz** ounce(s)

**pc** popcorn(s)

**rem** remain/remains/remaining

**rep(s)** repeat(s)

**rnd(s)** round(s)

**RS** right side

**sc** single crochet

**sc dec** single crochet 2 or more stitches together, as indicated

**sk** skip/skipped/skipping

**sl st(s)** slip stitch(es)

**sp(s)** space(s)/spaced

**st(s)** stitch(es)

**tog** together

**tr** treble crochet

**trtr** triple treble crochet

**WS** wrong side

**yd(s)** yard(s)

**yo** yarn over

## Symbols

**\* An asterisk** is used to mark the beginning of a portion of instructions which will be worked more than once; thus, "rep from \* twice" means after working the instructions once, repeat the instructions following the asterisk twice more (3 times in all).

**[ ] Brackets** are used to enclose instructions which should be repeated the number of times specified immediately following the brackets: "[2 sc in next dc, sc in next dc] twice." Brackets are also used to indicate additional or clarifying information for multiple sizes: "child's size 2 [4, 6]"; "Row 29 [31, 33]."

**( ) Parentheses** are used to set off and clarify a group of stitches that are to be worked all into the same space or stitch, such as: "in corner sp work (2 dc, ch 1, 2 dc)."

**{ } Braces** are used to indicate a set of repeat instructions within a bracketed or parenthetical set of repeat instructions: "[{ch 5, sc in next ch sp} twice, ch 5, sk next dc]"; "({dc, ch 1} 5 times, dc) in next ch sp)."

## Terms

**Front loop (front lp)** is the loop toward you at the top of the stitch (Figure 1).

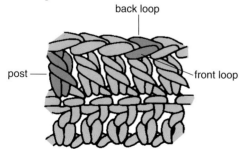

**Figure 1**

**Back loop (back lp)** is the loop away from you at the top of the stitch (Figure 1).

**Post** is the vertical part of the stitch (Figure 1).

**Wrong side (WS):** the side of the work that will not show when project is in use.

**Right side (RS):** the side that will show when project is in use.

## Gauge

Gauge is the single most important factor in crochet. If you don't work to gauge, your crocheted projects may not be the correct size, and you may not have enough yarn to finish your project.

Gauge means the number of stitches per inch, and the number of rows per inch, that result from a specified yarn worked with a specified-size hook. Since everyone crochets differently—loosely, tightly or in-between—the measurements of individual work can vary greatly even when using the same-size hook and yarn. It is your responsibility to make sure you achieve the gauge specified in the pattern.

Hook sizes given in the materials are merely guides and should never be used without making a 4-inch-square sample swatch to check gauge. Make the sample gauge swatch using the size hook, yarn and stitch specified in the pattern. If you have more stitches per inch than specified, try again using a larger-size hook. If you have fewer stitches per inch than specified, try again using a smaller-size hook. Do not hesitate to change to a larger- or smaller-size hook, if necessary, to achieve gauge.

If you have the correct number of stitches per inch, but cannot achieve the row gauge, adjust the height of your stitches. This means that after inserting the hook to begin a new stitch, you should draw up a little more yarn if your stitches are not tall enough—this makes the first loop slightly higher—or draw up less yarn if your stitches are too tall. Practice will help you achieve the correct height.

This photo shows how to measure your gauge:

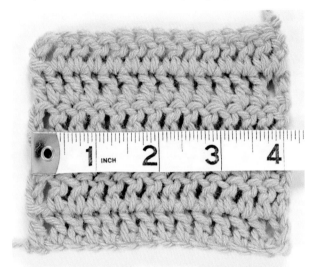

# Increasing & Decreasing

Shaping is done by increasing, which adds stitches to make the crocheted piece wider, or decreasing, which subtracts stitches to make the piece narrower.

*Tip: Make a practice sample by chaining 15 stitches loosely and working four rows of single crochet with 14 stitches in each row. Do not fasten off at end of last row. Use this sample swatch to practice the following method of increasing stitches.*

## Increasing

To increase one stitch in single, half double, double or treble crochet, simply work two stitches in one stitch. For example, if you are working in single crochet and you need to increase one stitch, you would work one single crochet in the next stitch; then you would work another single crochet in the same stitch.

*For practice:* On sample swatch, turn work and chain one. Single crochet in first two stitches; increase in next stitch by working two single crochet in stitch (Figure 2).

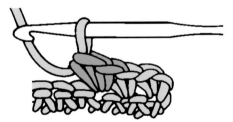

**Figure 2**
Single Crochet Increase

Repeat increase in each stitch across row to last two stitches; single crochet in each of next two stitches. Count your stitches: You should have 24 stitches. If you don't have 24 stitches, examine your swatch to see if you have increased in each specified stitch. Rework the row if necessary.

Increases in half double, double and treble crochet are shown in Figures 2a, 2b and 2c.

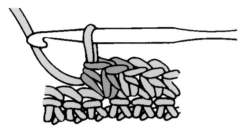

**Figure 2a**
Half Double Crochet Increase

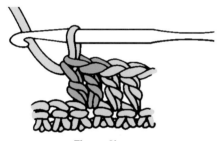

**Figure 2b**
Double Crochet Increase

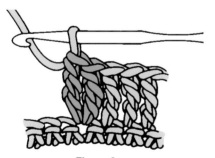

**Figure 2c**
Treble Crochet Increase

*Tip: Make another practice sample by chaining 15 loosely and working four rows of single crochet. Do not fasten off at end of last row. Use this sample swatch to practice the following methods of decreasing stitches.*

## Decreasing

This is how to work a decrease in the four main stitches. Each decrease gives one fewer stitch than you had before.

**Single crochet decrease (sc dec):** Insert hook and draw up a loop in each of the next two stitches (three loops now on hook), hook yarn and draw through all three loops on the hook (Figure 3).

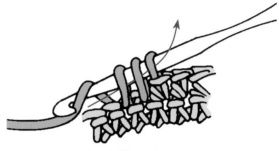

**Figure 3**

Single crochet decrease made (Figure 4).

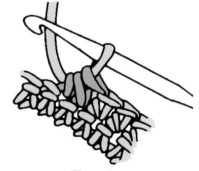

**Figure 4**

**Double crochet decrease (dc dec):** Work a double crochet in the specified stitch until two loops remain on the hook (Figure 5).

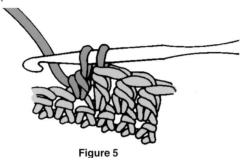

**Figure 5**

Keeping these two loops on hook, work another double crochet in the next stitch until three loops remain on hook; hook yarn and draw through all three loops on the hook (Figure 6).

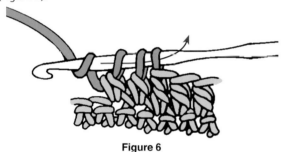

**Figure 6**

Double crochet decrease made (Figure 7).

**Figure 7**

**Half double crochet decrease (hdc dec):** Yo, insert hook in specified stitch and draw up a loop: three loops on the hook (Figure 8).

**Figure 8**

Keeping these three loops on hook, yo and draw up a loop in the next stitch (five loops now on hook), hook yarn and draw through all five loops on the hook (Figure 9).

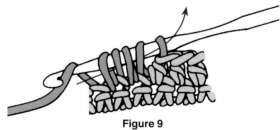

**Figure 9**

Half double crochet decrease made (Figure 10).

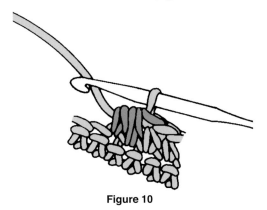

**Figure 10**

**Treble crochet decrease (tr dec):** Work a treble crochet in the specified stitch until two loops remain on the hook (Figure 11).

**Figure 11**

Keeping these two loops on hook, work another treble crochet in the next stitch until 3 loops remain on the hook; hook yarn and draw through all three loops on the hook (Figure 12).

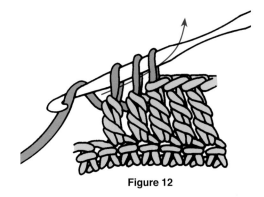

**Figure 12**

Treble crochet decrease made (Figure 13).

**Figure 13**

# Joining New Yarn

Never tie or leave knots! In crochet, yarn ends can be easily worked in and hidden because of the density of the stitches. Always leave at least 6 inches when fastening off yarn just used and when joining new yarn. If a flaw or a knot appears in the yarn while you are working from a skein, cut out the imperfection and rejoin the yarn.

Whenever possible, join new yarn at the end of a row. To do this, work the last stitch with the old yarn until two loops remain on the hook, and then use the new yarn complete the stitch (Figure 14).

To join new yarn in the middle of a row, when about 12 inches of the old yarn remains, work several more stitches with the old yarn, working the stitches over the end of new yarn (Figure 15, shown in double crochet). Then, change yarns in the next stitch as previously explained.

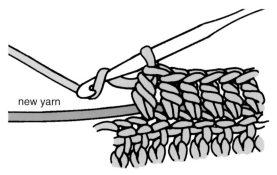

new yarn

**Figure 15**

Continuing with the new yarn, work the following stitches over the old yarn end.

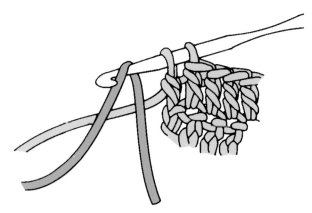

**Figure 14**

# Working With Colours

Working with colours often involves reading charts, changing colours and learning how to carry or pick up colours.

## Working From Charts

Charts are easy to work from once you understand how to follow them. When working from a chart, remember that for each odd-numbered row, you will work the chart from right to left, and for each even-numbered row, you will work the chart from left to right.

Odd-numbered rows are worked on the right side of the piece and even-numbered rows are worked on the wrong side. To help follow across the row, you will find it helpful to place a ruler or sheet of paper directly below the row being worked.

## Changing Colours

To change from working colour to a new colour, work the last stitch to be done in the working colour until two loops remain on the hook (Photo A). Draw new colour through the two loops on hook. Drop working colour (Photo B) and continue to work in the new colour. This method can be used when change of colour is at the end of a row or within the row.

**Photo A**

**Photo B**

## Carrying or Picking Up Colours

In some patterns, you may need to carry a colour on the wrong side of the work for several stitches or pick up a colour used on the previous row. To carry a colour means to carry the strand on the wrong side of the work. To prevent having loops of unworked yarn, it is helpful to work over the strand of the carried colour. To do this, consider the strand a part of the stitch being worked into and simply insert the hook in the stitch and draw the new colour through (Photo C). When changing from working colour to a colour that has been carried or used on the previous row, always bring this colour under the working colour. This is very important, as it prevents holes in your work.

**Photo C**

# Finishing & Edging

## Finishing

A carefully crocheted project can be disappointing if the finishing is done incorrectly. Correct finishing techniques are not difficult, but they do require time, attention and knowledge of basic techniques.

## Weaving in Ends

The first procedure of finishing is to securely weave in all yarn ends. Thread a size 16 steel tapestry needle with yarn end, and then weave running stitches either horizontally or vertically on the wrong side of work. First, weave about 1 inch in one direction and then ½ inch in the reverse direction. Be sure yarn doesn't show on right side of work. Cut off excess yarn. Never weave in more than one yarn end at a time.

## Sewing Seams

In order to avoid bulk, edges in crochet are usually butted together for seaming, instead of layered. Do not sew too tightly—seams should be elastic and have the same stretch as the crocheted pieces.

Carefully matching stitches and rows as much as possible, sew the seams with the same yarn you used when crocheting.

**Invisible seam:** This seam provides a smooth, neat appearance because the edges are woven together invisibly from the right side. Join vertical edges, such as side or sleeve seams, through the matching edge stitches, bringing the yarn up through the posts of the stitches (Figure 16).

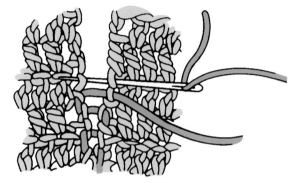

**Figure 16**

If a firmer seam is desired, weave the edges together through both the tops and the posts of the matching edge stitches.

**Backstitch seam:** This method gives a strong, firm edge and is used when the seam will have a lot of stress or pull on it. Hold the pieces with right sides together and then sew through both thicknesses as shown (Figure 17).

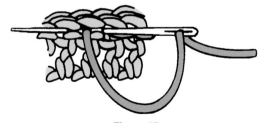

**Figure 17**

**Overcast seam:** Strips and pieces of afghans are frequently joined in this manner. Hold the pieces with right sides together and overcast edges, carefully matching stitches on the two pieces (Figure 18).

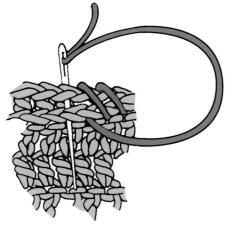

**Figure 18**

Edges can also be joined in this manner, using only the back loops or the front loops of each stitch (see page 8).

**Crocheted Seam:** Holding pieces with right sides together, join yarn with a slip stitch at right-side edge. Loosely slip stitch pieces together, being sure not to pull stitches too tightly (Figure 19). You may wish to use a hook one size larger than the one used in the project.

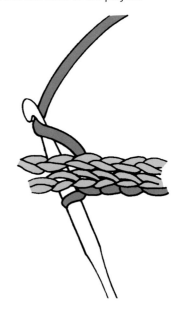

**Figure 19**

## Edging

### Single Crochet Edging

A round of single crochet worked around a completed project gives a finished look. The instructions will say to "work a round of single crochet, taking care to keep work flat." This means you need to adjust your stitches as you work. To work the edging, insert hook from front to back through the edge stitch and work a single crochet. Continue evenly along the edge. You may need to skip a row or a stitch here or there to keep the edging from rippling, or add a stitch to keep the work from pulling.

When working around a corner, it is usually necessary to work at least three stitches in the corner centre stitch to keep the corner flat and square (Figure 20).

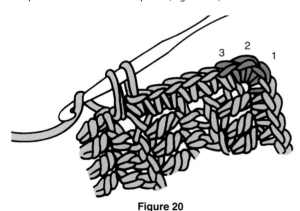

**Figure 20**

### Reverse Single Crochet Edging

A single crochet edging is sometimes worked from left to right for a more dominant edge. To work reverse single crochet, insert hook in stitch to the right (Figure 21), hook yarn and draw through stitch, hook yarn and draw through both loops on the hook (Figure 22).

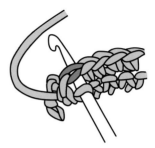

**Figure 21**

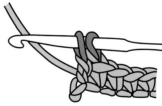

**Figure 22**

# SUNDAY PINK

*A little crochet and a purchased top make a dress perfect for your little one. Just add crocheted accessories and she is set to go.*

Design | Lucille LaFlamme

**Skill Level**  **EASY**

## Finished Sizes
Hat: 16 inches in circumference, excluding brim
Dress: Instructions given fit size 12 months
  (9 inches long from waist)
Purse: 6 inches x 6½ inches, excluding handle

# Hat

## Materials
Worsted weight yarn (256 yds/142g per ball):
  1 ball baby pink
Size F/5/3.75mm crochet hook or size needed to
  obtain gauge
Tapestry needle
Sewing needle
1 yd ¼-inch-wide white ribbon
1 white satin ribbon rose
Matching sewing thread

## Gauge
5 sc = 1 inch
Take time to check gauge.

## Notes
Weave in ends as work progresses.

Join with slip stitch as indicated unless
otherwise stated.

Chain-3 at beginning of row counts as first double crochet unless otherwise stated.

## Special Stitch
Picot: Ch 3, sl st in last st made.

## Hat
Rnd 1 (RS): Ch 3, join *(see Notes)* in first ch to form a ring, ch 3 *(see Notes)*, 16 dc in ring, join in 3rd ch of beg ch-3. *(17 dc)*

Rnd 2: Ch 3, dc in same ch as joining, 2 dc in each dc around, join in 3rd ch of beg ch-3. *(34 dc)*

**Sunday Pink**
Sample projects were crocheted with
Red Heart Soft Baby Steps (100 per
cent acrylic) from Coats & Clark.

**Rnd 3:** Ch 3, dc in same ch as joining, 2 dc in next dc, *dc in next dc, 2 dc in each of next 2 dc, rep from * around to last 2 dc, dc in each of last 2 dc, join in 3rd ch of beg ch-3. *(56 dc)*

**Rnd 4:** Ch 3, dc in each of next 3 dc, *2 dc in next dc, dc in each of next 4 dc, rep from * around to last 2 dc, 2 dc in next dc, dc in last dc, join in 3rd ch of beg ch-3. *(67 dc)*

**Rnd 5:** Ch 3, dc in each of next 7 dc, *2 dc in next dc, dc in each of next 4 dc, rep from * around to last 2 dc, 2 dc in next dc, dc in last dc, join in 3rd ch of beg ch-3. *(78 dc)*

**Rnd 6:** Ch 3, dc in each dc around, join in 3rd ch of beg ch-3.

**Rnd 7:** Ch 3, dc in each of next 4 dc, **dc dec** *(see Stitch Guide on page 126)* in next 2 dc, *dc in each of next 5 dc, dc dec next 2 dc, rep from * around to last dc, dc in last dc, join in 3rd ch of beg ch-3.

**Rnds 8 & 9:** Rep rnd 6.

### Brim

**Rnd 10:** Ch 3, dc in each of next 3 dc, *2 dc in next dc, dc in each of next 3 dc, rep from * around, join in 3rd ch of beg ch-3. *(84 dc)*

**Rnd 11:** Ch 3, dc in each of next 3 dc, *2 dc in next dc, dc in each of next 3 dc, rep from * around, join in 3rd ch of beg ch-3. *(104 dc)*

**Rnd 12:** Ch 3, [2 dc in next dc, dc in each of next 3 dc] 25 times, 2 dc in next dc, dc in each of next 2 dc, join in 3rd ch of beg ch-3. *(130 dc)*

**Rnd 13:** Ch 1, sc in same ch as joining, **picot** *(see Special Stitch)*, ch 3, sk next 2 dc, *sc in next dc, picot, ch 3, sk next 2 dc, rep from * around, join in first sc. Fasten off.

### Flower

Ch 4, join in first ch to form a ring, [ch 3, dc in ring, ch 3, sl st in ring] 5 times. Fasten off.

### Finishing

Sew white silk ribbon rose to centre of Flower. Sew Flower to top of Hat.

Cut 27-inch length of ribbon. Weave through rnd 8 and tie in bow.

# Dress

## Materials

Worsted weight yarn (256 yds/142g per ball):
   1 ball baby pink
Size F/5/3.75mm crochet hook or size needed
   to obtain gauge
Tapestry needle
Sewing needle
Purchased 12-month-old size white I-shirt
Matching sewing thread

## Gauge

6 sc = 1 inch
Take time to check gauge.

## Notes

Weave in ends as work progresses.

Join with slip stitch as indicated unless otherwise stated.

Chain-3 at beginning of round counts as first double crochet unless otherwise stated.

Chain-5 at beginning of round counts as first double crochet and chain-2 space unless otherwise stated.

## Special Stitches

**Beginning cluster (beg cl):** Ch 3, keeping back last lp of each dc, 2 dc in indicated sp, yo and draw through all 3 lps on hook.

**Cluster (cl):** Keeping back last lp of each dc, 3 dc in indicated st, yo and draw through all 4 lps on hook.

**Picot:** Ch 3, sl st in last st made.

## Skirt

**Rnd 1 (RS):** Ch 100, **join** *(see Notes)* in first ch, being careful not to twist ch, sc in same ch as joining, sc in each rem ch around, join in beg sc. *(100 sc)*

**Rnd 2:** Ch 1, 3 sc in first sc, *sc in each of next 3 sc, 2 sc in next sc, rep from * around to last 3 sc, sc in each of last 3 sc, join in beg sc. *(126 sc)*

**Rnd 3:** Ch 3, sk next 5 sc, *(dc, ch 1, dc, ch 3, dc, ch 1, dc) in next sc, sk next 5 sc, rep from * 19 times, (dc, ch 1, dc, ch 3, dc, ch 1) in same sc as beg ch-3, join in 3rd ch of beg ch-3.

**Rnd 4:** Sl st in next dc, sl st in next ch-1 sp, sl st in next ch-3 sp, **beg cl** *(see Special Stitches)* in same sp, ch 3, **cl** *(see Special Stitches)* in same sp, ch 3, *(cl, ch 3, cl) in next ch-3 sp, ch 3, rep from * around, join in top of beg cl.

**Rnd 5:** Sl st in next ch-3 sp, beg cl in same sp, ch 2, dc in next ch-3 sp, ch 2, *cl in next ch-3 sp, ch 2, dc in next ch-3 sp, ch 2, rep from * around, join in top of beg cl.

**Rnd 6:** Ch 5 *(see Notes)*, (dc, ch 1, dc) in next dc, ch 2, *dc in next cl, ch 2, (dc, ch 1, dc) in next dc, ch 2, rep from * around, join in 3rd ch of beg ch-5.

**Rnd 7:** Sl st in each of next 4 chs, sl st in next dc, sl st in next ch-1 sp, ch 4, (dc, ch 3, dc, ch 1, dc) in same sp, ch 1, sk next 2 ch-2 sps, *(dc, ch 1, dc, ch 3, dc, ch 1, dc) in next ch-1 sp, ch 1, sk next 2 ch-2 sps, rep from * around, join in 3rd ch of beg ch-4.

**Rnd 8:** Sl st in next ch, sl st in next dc, sl st in next ch-3 sp, (beg cl, ch 3, cl) in same sp, ch 3, *(cl, ch 3, cl) in next ch-3 sp, ch 3, rep from * around, join in top of beg cl.

**Rnd 9:** Sl st in next ch-3 sp, beg cl in same sp, ch 3, dc in next ch-3 sp, ch 3, *cl in next ch-3 sp, ch 3, dc in next ch-3 sp, ch 3, rep from * around, join in top of beg cl.

**Rnd 10:** Ch 5, (dc, ch 2, dc) in next dc, ch 2, *dc in next cl, ch 2, (dc, ch 2, dc) in next dc, ch 2, rep from * around, join in 3rd ch of beg ch-5.

**Rnd 11:** Sl st in each of next 2 chs, sl st in next dc, sl st in next ch-2 sp, ch 4, (dc, ch 3, dc, ch 1, dc) in same sp, ch 1, sk next 2 ch-2 sps, *(dc, ch 1, dc, ch 3, dc, ch 1, dc) in next ch-2 sp, ch 1, sk next 2 ch-2 sps, rep from * around, join in 3rd ch of beg ch-4.

**Rnds 12–15:** Rep rnds 8 to 11.

**Rnds 16–17:** Rep rnds 8 and 9.

## Edging

**Rnd 1 (RS):** Ch 1, sc in same beg cl, ch 3, dc in next dc, ch 3, *sc in next cl, ch 3, dc in next dc, ch 3, rep from * around, join in beg sc.

**Rnd 2:** Ch 1, sc in same sc as joining, ch 1, (hdc, ch 1, dc) in next ch-3 sp, ch 1, (dc, **picot**—*see Special Stitches*, dc) in next dc, ch 1, (dc, ch 1, hdc) in next ch-3 sp, ch 1, *sc in next sc, ch 1, (hdc, ch 1, dc) in next ch-3 sp, ch 1, (dc, picot, dc) in next dc, ch 1, (dc, ch 1, hdc) in next ch-3 sp, ch 1, rep from * around, join in beg sc. Fasten off.

## Collar Trim

Crochet a chain to measure around collar of T-shirt plus ½ inch, having a multiple of 6, (dc, ch 1, dc, picot, dc, ch 1, dc) in 4th ch from hook, ch 1, sk next 2 chs, sc in next ch, ch 1, sk next 2 chs, *(dc, ch 1, dc, picot, dc, ch 1, dc) in next ch, ch 1, sk next 2 chs, sc in next ch, ch 1, sk next 2 chs, rep from * across to last 2 chs, (dc, ch 1, dc, picot, dc, ch 1, dc) in next ch, ch 1, sc in last ch. Fasten off.

## Sleeve Trim
**Make 2**

Crochet a chain to measure around sleeve of T-shirt plus ½ inch, having a multiple of 6, (dc, ch 1, dc, picot, dc, ch 1, dc) in 4th ch from hook, ch 1, sk next 2 chs, sc in next ch, ch 1, sk next 2 chs, *(dc, ch 1, dc, picot, dc, ch 1, dc) in next ch, ch 1, sk next 2 chs, sc in next ch, ch 1, sk next 2 chs, rep from * across to last 2 chs, (dc, ch 1, dc, picot, dc, ch 1, dc) in next ch, ch 1, sc in last ch. Fasten off.

## Finishing
Sew Skirt, Collar Trim and Sleeve Trims to T-shirt.

# Purse

## Materials
Worsted weight yarn (256 yds/142g per ball):
   1 ball baby pink
Size F/5/3.75mm crochet hook or size needed
   to obtain gauge
Tapestry needle
Sewing needle
1 yd ¼-inch-wide white ribbon
Matching sewing thread

**4 MEDIUM**

## Gauge
Rnd 1 = 1 inch
Take time to check gauge.

## Notes
Weave in ends as work progresses.

Join with slip stitch as indicated unless otherwise stated.

Chain-3 at beginning of round counts as first double crochet unless otherwise stated.

Chain-5 at beginning of round counts as first double crochet and chain-2 space unless otherwise stated.

## Special Stitches
**Beginning cluster (beg cl):** Ch 3, keeping back last lp of each dc, 2 dc in indicated sp, yo and draw through all 3 lps on hook.

**Cluster (cl):** Keeping back last lp of each dc, 3 dc in indicated st, yo and draw through all 4 lps on hook.

**Picot:** Ch 3, sl st in last st made.

## Purse
**Rnd 1 (RS):** Ch 3, join *(see Notes)* in first ch to form a ring, **ch 3** *(see Notes)*, 16 dc in ring, join in 3rd ch of beg ch-3. *(17 dc)*

**Rnd 2:** Ch 3, dc in same ch as joining, 2 dc in each dc around, join in 3rd ch of beg ch-3. *(34 dc)*

**Rnd 3:** Ch 3, dc in same ch as joining, 2 dc in next dc, *dc in next dc, 2 dc in each of next 2 dc, rep from * around to last 2 dc, dc in each of last 2 dc, join in 3rd ch of beg ch-3. *(56 dc)*

**Rnd 4:** Ch 3, dc in each of next 3 dc, *2 dc in next dc, dc in each of next 4 dc, rep from * around to last 2 dc, 2 dc in next dc, dc in last dc, join in 3rd ch of beg ch-3. *(67 dc)*

**Rnd 5:** Ch 3, dc in each of next 7 dc, *2 dc in next dc, dc in each of next 4 dc, rep from * around to last 2 dc, 2 dc in next dc, dc in last dc, join in 3rd ch of beg ch-3. *(78 dc)*

**Rnd 6:** Ch 3, dc in each of next 11 dc, *dc dec *(see Stitch Guide on page 126)* in next 2 dc, dc in each of next 12 dc, rep from * 3 times, dc dec in next 2 dc, dc in each of next 6 dc, dc dec in last 2 dc, join in 3rd ch of beg ch-3. *(72 dc)*

**Rnd 7:** Ch 3, dc in each dc around, join in 3rd ch of beg ch-3.

**Rnds 8 & 9:** Rep rnd 7.

**Rnd 10:** Ch 1, sc in each dc around, join in beg sc.

## Border

**Rnd 11:** Ch 3, sk next 5 sc, *(dc, ch 1, dc, ch 3, dc, ch 1, dc) in next sc, sk next 5 sc, rep from * 10 times, (dc, ch 1, dc, ch 3, dc, ch 1) in same sc as beg ch-3, join in 3rd ch of beg ch-3.

**Rnd 12:** Sl st in next dc, sl st in next ch-1 sp, sl st in next ch-3 sp, (**beg cl**—*see Special Stitches*, ch 3, **cl**—*see Special Stitches*) in same sp, ch 3, *(cl, ch 3, cl) in next ch-3 sp, ch 3, rep from * around, join in top of beg cl.

**Rnd 13:** Sl st in next ch-3 sp, beg cl in same sp, ch 2, dc in next ch-3 sp, ch 2, *cl in next ch-3 sp, ch 2, dc in next ch-3 sp, ch 2, rep from * around, join in top of beg cl.

**Rnd 14:** Ch 5 *(see Notes)*, (dc, ch 1, dc) in next dc, ch 2, *dc in next cl, ch 2, (dc, ch 1, dc) in next dc, ch 2, rep from * around, join in 3rd ch of beg ch-5.

**Rnd 15:** Ch 1, sc in same ch as joining, ch 3, *dc in next ch-1 sp, ch 3, sk next dc, sc in next dc, ch 3, rep from * around, join in beg sc.

**Rnd 16:** Ch 1, sc in same sc as joining, ch 1, (hdc, ch 1, dc) in next ch-3 sp, ch 1, (dc, **picot**—*see Special Stitches*, dc) in next dc, ch 1, (dc, ch 1, hdc) in next ch-3 sp, ch 1, *sc in next sc, ch 1, (hdc, ch 1, dc) in next ch-3 sp, ch 1, (dc, picot, dc) in next dc, ch 1, (dc, ch 1, hdc) in next ch-3 sp, ch 1, rep from * around, join in beg sc. Fasten off.

## Handle

**Row 1 (RS):** Ch 7, dc in 4th ch from hook *(beg 3 sk chs count as a dc)*, dc in each of next 3 chs, turn. *(5 dc)*

**Row 2:** Ch 3, dc in each of next 4 dc, turn.

**Rows 3–19:** Rep row 2. At end of last row, fasten off.

## Finishing

Cut a 25-inch length of ribbon. Weave ribbon through ch-1 spaces of rnd 14. Gather slightly and tie in a bow. Sew ends of Handle to sides of Purse. ■

# BABY SET

*Dress your little one from head to toe*
*in this adorable Sunday outfit.*

Design | Sue Childress

## Skill Level

## Finished Sizes

Instructions given fit size 0–3 months, 6–9 months or 9–12 months, depending on size of hook used.

## Materials

Chenille sport weight yarn (88 yds/per ball):
    9 [10, 12] balls dark pink, 2 [2, 2] balls ivory
4 off-white 8mm pearl buttons
Off-white sewing thread
Sewing and tapestry needle
Size D/3/3.25mm crochet hook (0–3 months), size
    E/4/3.5mm crochet hook (6–9 months) or size
    F/5/3.75mm crochet hook (9–12 months), or size
    needed to obtain gauge

## Gauge

**Size D hook:** 11 sc = 2 inches; 11 dc rows = 4 inches; 9 cl
    rows = 4 inches
**Size E hook:** 5 sc = 1 inch; 5 dc rows = 2 inches; 2 cl rows
    = 1 inch
**Size F hook:** 9 sc = 2 inches; 9 dc rows = 4 inches; 7 cl
    rows = 4 inches
Take time to check gauge.

## Special Stitches

**Beginning cluster (beg cl):** Ch 3, [yo, insert hook in same st or sp, yo, draw lp through, yo, draw through 2 lps on hook] 2 times, yo, draw through all 3 lps on hook.

**Cluster (cl):** Yo, insert hook in next st or sp, yo, draw lp through, yo, draw through 2 lps on hook, [yo, insert hook in same st, yo, draw lp through, yo, draw through 2 lps on hook] 2 times, yo, draw through all 4 lps on hook.

**Beginning cluster shell (beg cl shell):** Beg cl, ch 2, cl in same sp.

**Cluster shell (cl shell):** (Cl, ch 2, cl) in next ch sp.

**Half double crochet back post (hdc bp):** Yo, insert hook from front to back around post of next st, yo, draw lp through, yo, draw through all 3 lps on hook.

## Dress

**Row 1:** Starting at **neck**, with dark pink, ch 69, sc in 2nd ch from hook, sc in each of next 2 chs, 2 sc in next ch, [sc in each of next 3 chs, 2 sc in next ch] across, turn. *(85 sc)*

**Row 2:** Ch 2, hdc in each st across, turn.

**Row 3:** Ch 3, dc in each of next 3 sts, 2 dc in next st, [dc in next 4 sts, 2 dc in next st] across, turn. *(102 dc)*

**Row 4:** Ch 3, dc in same st, [dc in next 4 sts, 2 dc in next st] across to last st, dc in last st, turn. *(123 dc)*

Baby Set
Sample projects were crocheted with
Honeysuckle Rayon Chenille (100 per
cent rayon) from Elmore Pisgah.

**Row 5:** Ch 3, dc in each st across, turn.

**Row 6:** Ch 3, dc in next st, ch 1, sk next st, **cl** *(see Special Stitches on page 26)* in next st, ch 1, sk next st, [dc in next st, ch 1, sk next st, cl in next st, ch 1, sk next st] across to last 2 sts, dc in each of last 2 sts, turn. *(60 ch-1 sps, 33 dc, 30 cls)*

**Row 7:** Ch 3, dc in next st, 3 dc in each ch sp across to last 2 sts, dc in each of last 2 sts, turn. *(184 dc)*

**Row 8:** Ch 3, dc in next 28 sts, [dc in next st, ch 2] 33 times, dc in next 60 sts, [ch 2, dc in next st] 33 times, dc in last 29 sts, turn. *(184 dc, 66 ch-2 sps)*

**Row 9:** Ch 3, dc in next 29 sts, for **armhole**, ch 4, sk next 33 ch sps, dc in next 60 sts, for **2nd armhole**, ch 4, sk next 33 ch sps, dc in last 30 sts, turn. *(120 dc)*

**Row 10:** Ch 3, dc in same st, dc in each st and in each ch across with 2 dc in last st, turn. *(130 dc)*

**Rnd 11:** Now working in rnds, ch 4, sk next st, cl in next st, ch 1, sk next st, [dc in each of next 2 sts, ch 1, sk next st, cl in next st, ch 1, sk next st] across to last st, dc in last st, join with sl st in 3rd ch of ch-4. *(52 dc, 52 ch-1 sps, 26 cls)*

**Rnd 12:** Sl st in next ch sp, ch 3, 2 dc in same sp, ch 1, cl in next ch sp, ch 1, (3 dc in next ch sp, ch 1, cl in next ch sp, ch 1) around, join with sl st in top of ch-3.

**Rnd 13:** Sl st in each of next 2 sts, sl st in next ch sp, **beg cl** *(see Special Stitches on page 26)*, ch 2, [cl in next ch sp, ch 2] around, join with sl st in top of beg cl.

**Rnds 14–16:** Sl st in next ch sp, beg cl, ch 2, [cl in next ch sp, ch 2] around, join.

**Rnd 17:** Sl st in next ch sp, **beg cl shell** *(see Special Stitches on page 26)*, ch 2, sk next ch sp, [**cl shell** *(see Special Stitches on page 26)* in next ch sp, ch 2, sk next ch sp] around, join. *(26 cl shells, 26 ch-2 sps)*

**Rnds 18–20:** Sl st in next ch sp, beg cl shell, ch 2, [cl shell in ch sp of next cl shell, ch 2] around, join.

**Rnds 21–23:** Sl st in next ch sp, beg cl, ch 2, [cl in next ch sp, ch 2] around, join. *(52 cls, 52 ch-2 sps)*

**Rnd 24:** Sl st in next ch sp, ch 3, 4 dc in same sp, ch 1, sk next ch sp, [5 dc in next ch sp, ch 1, sk next ch sp] around, join with sl st in top of ch-3. *(26 5-dc groups, 26 ch-1 sps)*

**Rnd 25:** Ch 3, dc in next st, 3 dc in next st, dc in each of next 2 sts, ch 1, sk next ch sp, [dc in each of next 2 sts, 3 dc in next st, dc in each of next 2 sts, ch 1, sk next ch sp] around, join. *(182 sts, 26 ch-1 sps)*

**Rnd 26:** Ch 3, dc in each of next 2 sts, 3 dc in next st, dc in each of next 3 sts, sc in next ch sp, [dc in each of next 3 sts, 3 dc in next st, dc in each of next 3 sts, sc in next ch sp] around, join, fasten off. *(260 sts)*

**Rnd 27:** Join ivory with sc in any st, ch 3, [sc in next st, ch 3] around, join with sl st in first sc, fasten off.

## Sleeve Trim

Working on 1 armhole in sk ch sps of rnd 8, join ivory with sc in first ch sp, [ch 3, sc in next ch sp] across, fasten off.

Rep on other armhole.

## Button & Buttonhole Plackets

**Row 1:** With RS of work facing you, working in ends of rows across back opening, join dark pink with sc in first row at neck edge, evenly sp 21 more sc across first side, evenly sp 22 sc across 2nd side, turn. *(44 sc)*

**Row 2:** Ch 1, sc in first 24 sts, [for **buttonhole**, ch 2, sk next 2 sts, sc in each of next 3 sts] 4 times, turn, fasten off.

**Row 3:** Join ivory with sc in first st, sc in each st and in each ch sp across, ch 3, [sc in end of next row, ch 3] 2 times, working in starting ch on opposite side of row 1 on neck edge, [sc in next ch, ch 3] across, [sc in end of next row, ch 3] 2 times, join with sl st in first sc, fasten off.

Sew buttons to Placket opposite buttonholes.

## Flower
### Make 2

**Rnd 1:** With ivory, ch 4, sl st in first ch to form ring, beg cl, ch 1, [cl in ring, ch 1] 5 times, join with sl st in top of beg cl. *(6 cls, 6 ch-1 sps)*

**Rnd 2:** Sl st in next ch sp, ch 1, (sc, ch 4, sc, ch 4, sc) in same sp and in each ch sp around, join with sl st in first sc, fasten off.

Sew 1 Flower to left front of bodice as shown in photo. Lay remaining Flower aside.

# Bootie
### Make 2

**Rnd 1:** Starting at **sole**, with dark pink, ch 10, hdc in 3rd ch from hook, hdc in next 6 chs, 5 dc in last ch, working on opposite side of ch, hdc in last 7 chs, join with sl st in top of ch-2. *(20 hdc)*

**Rnd 2:** Ch 2, hdc in same st, 2 hdc in next st, hdc in next 7 sts, 2 hdc in each of next 4 sts, hdc in next 6 sts, 2 hdc in last st, join. *(27 hdc)*

**Rnd 3:** Ch 1, sc in first st, 2 sc in next st, sc in next 10 sts, hdc in next st, 3 dc in next st, [2 dc in next st, 3 dc in next st] 2 times, hdc in next st, sc in last 8 sts, join with sl st in first sc. *(36 sts)*

**Rnd 4:** Ch 1, sc in first 16 sts, 2 hdc in next st, [hdc in next st, 2 hdc in next st] 3 times, sc in last 13 sts, join. *(40 sts)*

**Rnd 5:** Ch 2, **hdc bp** *(see Special Stitches on page 26)* around each st around, join with sl st in top of ch-2.

**Rnd 6:** Beg cl, ch 1, sk next st, [cl in next st, ch 1, sk next st] around, join with sl st in top of beg cl. *(20 cls, 20 ch-1 sps)*

**Rnd 7:** Sl st in next ch sp, ch 1, 2 sc in same sp and in each of next 6 ch sps, sc in next 7 ch sps, 2 sc in each of last 6 ch sps, join with sl st in first sc. *(33 sc)*

**Rnd 8:** Ch 1, sc in first 13 sts, [sc next 2 sts tog] 5 times, sc in last 10 sts, join. *(28 sc)*

**Rnd 9:** Ch 1, sc in first 12 sts, [sc next 2 sts tog] 3 times, sc in last 10 sts, join, fasten off.

### Ties
#### Make 2

With ivory, ch 75, fasten off. Starting at centre front, weave through sts of rnd 8, tie ends into a bow.

# Bonnet

**Rnd 1:** With dark pink, ch 4, sl st in first ch to form ring, **beg cl** *(see Special Stitches on page 26)* in ring, ch 2, [cl *(see Special Stitches on page 26)* in ring, ch 2] 4 times, join with sl st in top of beg cl. *(5 ch-2 sps)*

**Rnds 2 & 3:** Sl st in next ch sp, **beg cl shell** *(see Special Stitches on page 26)*, ch 2, [cl shell *(see Special Stitches on page 26)* in next ch sp, ch 2] around, join, ending with 10 cl shells and 10 ch-2 sps in last rnd.

**Rnd 4:** Sl st in next ch sp, beg cl shell, ch 2, cl in next ch sp, ch 2, [cl shell in next ch sp, ch 2, cl in next ch sp, ch 2] around, join. *(20 ch-2 sps, 10 cls shells, 10 cls)*

**Rnds 5–9:** Sl st in next ch sp, beg cl, ch 2, [cl in next ch sp, ch 2] around, join. *(30 cls, 30 ch-2 sps)*

*Note: Do not join the following rnds unless otherwise stated. Mark first st of each rnd.*

**Rnd 10:** Sl st in next ch sp, ch 1, 2 sc in same sp, 2 sc in each ch sp around. *(60 sc)*

**Rnds 11–13:** Sc in each st around. At end of last rnd, join with sl st in first sc, fasten off.

**Rnd 14:** Join ivory with sc in first st, ch 3, [sc in next st, ch 3] around, join, fasten off.

Sew rem Flower over rnd 12. ∎

# TEDDY & ME BIBS

*Dress baby and teddy alike in these beautiful crocheted bibs.*

Design | Elizabeth Ann White

**Skill Level**
**EASY**

**Finished Sizes**
Infant's Bib: fits 6–12 months
Teddy's Bib: fits 12-inch teddy bear

**Materials**
Size 10 crochet cotton (350 yds per ball):
   1 ball each cream and rose, small amount green
2⅔ yds ⅜-inch-wide pink ribbon
Sewing needle and thread
Size 7/1.65mm steel crochet hook or size needed to obtain gauge

**Gauge**
8 dc = 1 inch; 4 dc rows = 1 inch
Take time to check gauge.

## Infant's Bib

**Row 1:** With cream, ch 65, dc in 8th ch from hook, [ch 2, sk next 2 chs, dc in next ch] across, turn. *(21 dc, 20 ch-2 sps made)*

**Row 2:** Ch 5 *(counts as first dc and ch-2)*, sk first ch sp, dc in next st, [2 dc in next ch sp, dc in next st] 18 times, ch 2, sk last ch sp, dc in last st, turn. *(57 dc, 2 ch-2 sps)*

*Note: Back of row 2 is RS of work.*

**Rows 3–21:** Ch 5, sk first ch sp, dc in each st across to last ch sp, ch 2, sk last ch sp, dc in last st, turn.

**Row 22:** Ch 5, sk first ch sp, dc in next 13 sts, [ch 2, sk next 2 sts, dc in next st] 10 times, dc in next 12 sts, ch 2, sk last ch sp, dc in last st, turn. *(37 dc, 12 ch sps)*

**Row 23:** For **first side**, ch 5, sk first ch sp, dc in next 13 sts, ch 2, sk next ch sp, dc in next st, leaving rem sts unworked, turn. *(15 dc, 2 ch sps)*

**Rows 24–29:** Ch 5, sk first ch sp, dc in next 13 sts, ch 2, sk last ch sp, dc in last st, turn.

**Row 30:** Ch 5, sk first ch sp, dc in next st, [ch 2, sk next 2 sts, dc in next st] 4 times, ch 2, sk last ch sp, dc in last st. Fasten off.

**Row 23:** For **2nd side**, with WS facing you, join with sl st in first st on opposite end of row 22, ch 5, sk first ch sp, dc in next 13 sts, ch 2, sk next ch sp, dc in next st, leaving rem sts unworked for neck edge, turn. *(15 dc, 2 ch sps)*

**Rows 24–29:** Ch 5, sk first ch sp, dc in next 13 sts, ch 2, sk last ch sp, dc in last st, turn.

**Row 30:** Ch 5, sk first ch sp, dc in next st, [ch 2, sk next 2 sts, dc in next st] 4 times, ch 2, sk last ch sp, dc in last st. Fasten off.

## Edging

**Row 1:** With RS facing you, join cream with sc in end of row 29 at neck edge on 2nd side, (ch 3, sc, ch 5, sc) in end of row 30 at corner, working in ch sps and in ends of rows, *ch 3, (sc in next ch sp or row, ch 5, sc in next ch sp or row, ch 3) across to next corner, (sc, ch 5, sc) in corner, rep from * 4 more times, ch 3, sc in end of row 29, leaving rem ch sps unworked, turn.

**Row 2:** Sl st in first 2 chs of first ch-3 sp, ch 1, sc in same ch sp, (ch 1, dc) 9 times in next corner ch-5 sp, [ch 1, sc in next ch-3 sp, *(ch 1, dc) 5 times in next ch-5 sp, ch 1, sc in next ch-3 sp, rep from * across to next corner ch-5 sp, (ch 1, dc) 9 times in corner ch-5 sp], rep between [ ] 4 more times, ch 1, sc in last ch sp, turn.

**Row 3:** Ch 3, sk next ch sp, [sc in next ch sp, ch 3] 8 times, sk next ch sp, sc in next sc, ch 3, work the following steps to complete the row:

**A:** *Sk next ch sp, [sc in next ch sp, ch 3] 4 times, sk next ch sp, sc in next sc, ch 3, rep from * across to next corner;

**B:** Sk next ch sp, [sc in next ch sp, ch 3] 8 times, sk next ch sp, sc in next sc, ch 3;

**C:** Rep steps A and B 4 times, sk next ch sp, sc in last sc. Fasten off.

## Large Rose

**Rnd 1:** With rose, ch 6, sl st in first ch to form ring, [sc in ring, ch 3] 5 times, join with sl st in first sc. *(5 ch sps made)*

**Rnd 2:** For **petals**, ch 1, (sc, hdc, 3 dc, hdc, sc) in each ch sp around, join with sl st in first sc. *(5 petals)*

**Rnd 3:** Ch 4, working behind petals, [sl st in sp between next 2 petals, ch 4] around, join with sl st in first ch of first ch-4.

**Rnd 4:** For **petals**, ch 1, (sc, hdc, 5 dc, hdc, sc) in each ch sp around, join with sl st in first sc.

**Rnd 5:** Ch 5, working behind petals, [sl st in sp between next 2 petals, ch 5] around, join with sl st in first ch of first ch-5.

**Rnd 6:** For **petals**, ch 1, (sc, hdc, 3 dc, tr, 3 dc, hdc, sc) in each ch sp around, join with sl st in first sc. Fasten off.

## Large Leaf
### Make 2

With green, ch 10, sc in 2nd ch from hook, *hdc in next ch, dc in next ch, tr in next 3 chs, dc in next ch, hdc in next ch*, 3 sc in last ch, working on opposite side of starting ch, rep between *, 2 sc in last ch, join with sl st in first sc. Fasten off.

Sew **back lps** *(see Stitch Guide on page 126)* of Rose and Leaves to centre front of Bib as shown in photo.

Cut 35 inches of ribbon, weave through sps around neck edge leaving ends for **ties**. Tie a knot in end of each ribbon.

Cut 26 inches of ribbon, weave through sps around outer edge of Bib, turn ends under and sew to base of Ties.

## Teddy & Me Bibs

Sample projects were crocheted with Aunt
Lydia's Classic Crochet Thread (100 per cent
mercerized cotton) from Coats & Clark.

# Teddy's Bib

**Row 1:** With cream, ch 35, dc in 8th ch from hook, [ch 2, sk next 2 chs, dc in next ch] across, turn. *(11 dc, 10 ch-2 sps made)*

**Row 2 (RS):** Ch 5 *(counts as first dc and ch-2)*, sk first ch sp, dc in next st, [2 dc in next ch sp, dc in next st] 8 times, ch 2, sk last ch sp, dc in last st, turn. *(27 dc, 2 ch-2 sps)*

*Note: Front of row 2 is RS of work.*

**Rows 3–11:** Ch 5, sk first ch sp, dc in each st across to last ch sp, ch 2, sk last ch sp, dc in last st, turn.

**Row 12:** For **first side**, ch 5, sk first ch sp, dc in next 4 sts, leaving rem sts unworked, turn. *(5 dc, 1 ch sp)*

**Row 13:** Ch 3, dc in next 3 sts, ch 2, sk next ch sp, dc in last st, turn.

**Row 14:** Ch 5, sk first ch sp, dc in last 4 sts, turn.

**Row 15:** Ch 3, dc in next 3 sts, ch 2, sk next ch sp, dc in last st, turn.

**Row 16:** Ch 5, sk first ch sp, dc in next st, ch 2, sk next 2 sts, dc in last st, turn. Fasten off.

**Row 12:** For **2nd side**, with WS facing you, join with sl st in first st on opposite end of row 11, ch 5, sk first ch sp, dc in next 4 sts, leaving rem sts unworked for neck edge, turn. *(5 dc, 1 ch sp)*

**Row 13:** Ch 3, dc in next 3 sts, ch 2, sk next ch sp, dc in last st, turn.

**Row 14:** Ch 5, sk first ch sp, dc in last 4 sts, turn.

**Row 15:** Ch 3, dc in next 3 sts, ch 2, sk next ch sp, dc in last st, turn.

**Row 16:** Ch 5, sk first ch sp, dc in next st, ch 2, sk next 2 sts, dc in last st. Fasten off.

## Edging

**Row 1:** With RS facing you, join cream with sc in end of row 16 on 2nd side at neck edge, (ch 3, sc, ch 5, sc, ch 3) in end of same row, (sc, ch 5, sc) in next ch sp at corner, working in ends of rows and in ch sps, *ch 3, [sc in next row or ch sp, ch 5, sc in next row or ch sp, ch 3] across to next corner, (sc, ch 5, sc) in ch sp at corner, rep from * 2 more times, ch 3, (sc, ch 5, sc, ch 3, sc) in opposite end of row 16, turn.

**Row 2:** Sl st in first 2 chs of first ch-3 sp, ch 1, sc in same ch sp, (ch 1, dc) 5 times in next corner ch-5 sp, ch 1, sc in next ch-3 sp, (ch 1, dc) 5 times in next corner ch-5 sp, [ch 1, sc in next ch-3 sp, *(ch 1, dc) 3 times in next ch-5 sp, ch 1, sc in next ch-3 sp, rep from * across to next corner ch-5 sp, (ch 1, dc) 5 times in corner ch-5 sp], rep between [ ] 2 more times, ch 1, sc in next ch-3 sp, (ch 1, dc) 5 times in next corner ch-5 sp, ch 1, sc in last ch-3 sp, turn.

**Row 3:** Ch 1, sc in first ch sp, (ch 3, sc in next ch sp) 5 times, (sc in next ch sp, ch 3) 5 times, *sc in next ch sp, (sc in next ch sp, ch 3) 3 times, rep from * across to next corner, sc in next ch sp, rep from * 2 more times, (sc in next ch sp, ch 3) 5 times, sc in next ch sp, (sc in next ch sp, ch 3) 5 times, sc in last ch sp. Fasten off.

*Note: Front of row 3 is RS of work.*

## Small Rose

**Rnd 1:** With rose, ch 6, sl st in first ch to form ring, (sc in ring, ch 3) 5 times, join with sl st in first sc. *(5 ch sps made)*

**Rnd 2:** For petals, ch 1, (sc, hdc, 3 dc, hdc, sc) in each ch sp around, join with sl st in first sc. Fasten off. *(5 petals)*

## Small Leaf
### Make 2

With green, ch 7, sc in 2nd ch from hook, hdc in next ch, dc in next 2 chs, hdc in next ch, 3 sc in last ch, working on opposite side of starting ch, hdc in next ch, dc in next 2 chs, hdc in next ch, 2 sc in last ch, join with sl st in first sc. Fasten off.

Sew **back lps** *(see Stitch Guide on page 126)* of Rose and Leaves to centre front of Bib as shown in photo.

Weave 35 inches of ribbon through sps around outer edge leaving ends for **ties**. Tie a knot in end of each ribbon. ■

# BEACH BABY ENSEMBLE

*Create a seaside sensation with this cute ensemble.*

Design | Mary Ann Sipes

## Skill Level

**INTERMEDIATE**

### Finished Sizes

Bikini Set: Instructions given fit size 3 months; changes for sizes 6, 12 and 18 months are in [ ].

Poncho: Instructions given fit size 3–6 months; changes for sizes 6–12 months and 12–18 months are in [ ].

### Materials

Worsted weight yarn (solids: 171 yds/100g; ombrés: 150 yds/85g per ball): 3 [3, 3, 3] balls blue (A), 1 [1, 1, 2] balls multicoloured (B)

Embroidery floss: small amount white (C), small amount yellow (D)

Sizes E/4/3.5mm and G/6/4mm crochet hooks or sizes needed to obtain gauge

Size 5/1.90mm steel crochet hook (for flower)

Tapestry needle

Stitch markers

Safety pin

1 yd ⅛-inch-wide elastic (for bikini top)

½ yd ½-inch-wide elastic (for panty)

Sewing needle and matching thread

### Gauge

**Size E hook:** 9 sc = 2 inches

**Size G hook:** 7 sc = 2 inches

Take time to check gauge.

## Bikini

### Halter Front

**Row 1 (RS):** With E hook and B, ch 10 [10, 12, 12], working in back bar only, sc in 2nd ch from hook and in each rem ch, turn. *(9 [9, 11, 11] sc)*

**Row 2:** Ch 1, working in back bar only, sc in each sc, turn. *(9 [9, 11, 11] sc)*

**Rows 3–30 [3–32, 3–34, 3–36]:** Rep row 2.

*Note: Place marker in first sc of last row to mark end of Halter Front.*

### Halter Back

**Row 1:** Ch 1, **sc dec** *(see Stitch Guide on page 126)* in first 2 sc, working in back lps only, sc in each rem sc, turn. *(8 [8, 10, 10] sc)*

**Row 2:** Ch 1, working in back lps only, sc in first 6 [6, 8, 8] sc, sc dec in last 2 sc, turn. *(7 [7, 9, 9] sc)*

**Row 3:** Ch 1, sc dec in first 2 sc, working in back lps only, sc in each rem sc, turn. *(6 [6, 8, 8] sc)*

**Row 4:** Ch 1, working in back lps only, sc in first 4 [4, 6, 6] sc, sc dec in last 2 sc, turn. *(5 [5, 7, 7] sc)*

**Row 5:** Rep row 2. *(4 [4, 6, 6] sc at end of row)*

**Beach Baby Ensemble**
Sample projects were crocheted with
Cottontots (100 per cent cotton) from
Bernat and embroidery floss from DMC.

**Row 6:** Ch 1, working in back lps only, sc in first 2 [2, 4, 4] sc, sc dec over last 2 sc, turn. *(3 [3, 5, 5] sc)*

**Row 7:** Ch 1, working in back lps only, sc in each sc, turn.

**Rows 8–24: [8–26, 8–28, 8–30]:** Rep row 7.

**Row 25 [27, 29, 31]:** Ch 1, working in back lps only, 2 sc in first sc, sc in each rem sc, turn. *(4 [4, 6, 6] sc)*

**Row 26 [28, 30, 32]:** Ch 1, working in back lps only, sc in first 3 [3, 5, 5] sc, 2 sc in last sc, turn. *(5 [5, 7, 7] sc)*

**Row 27 [29, 31, 33]:** Rep row 25 [27, 29, 31]. *(6 [6, 8, 8] sc at end of row)*

**Row 28 [30, 32, 34]:** Ch 1, working in back lps only, sc in first 5 [5, 7, 7] sc, 2 sc in last sc, turn. *(7 [7, 9, 9] sc)*

**Row 29 [31, 33, 35]:** Rep row 25 [27, 29, 31]. *(8 [8, 10, 10] sc at end of row)*

**Row 30 [32, 34, 36]:** Ch 1, working in back lps only, sc in first 7 [7, 9, 9] sc, 2 sc in last sc. *(9 [9, 11, 11] sc)*

Fasten off, leaving an 8-inch end for sewing. Weave in other end.

## Assembly

Hold beg and end of Halter with WS tog, with tapestry needle and long end left for sewing, and working in back lps of sc only, sew ends tog through back lps only of corresponding sc.

## Lower Casing

**Rnd 1:** Hold piece with RS facing you and 1 long edge at top, with E hook, join A with sl st in end of centre row of Halter Back, ch 1, sc in same sp as joining, working in ends of rem rows, sc in each row, join with sl st in first sc.

**Rnd 2:** Ch 1, sc in same sc and in each rem sc, join with sl st in first sc. Fasten off.

Fold last rnd toward WS of piece. With tapestry needle and A, sew to 2nd row below to form casing. Leave small opening for threading elastic through casing.

## Top Casing

**Rnd 1:** Hold piece with RS facing you and unworked long edge at top, with E hook, join A with sl st in end of centre row of Halter Back, ch 1, sc in same sp as joining, ch 1, working in ends of rows, *sk next row, sc in next row, ch 1, rep from * around, join with sl st in **front lp** *(see Stitch Guide on page 126)* of first sc.

**Rnd 2:** Ch 1, sc in same sc, working in front lps only, sc in each ch and in each rem sc, join with sl st in back lp of first sc.

**Rnd 3:** Ch 1, sc in lp as joining and in back lp of each rem sc, join with sl st in back lp of first sc.

Fasten off, leaving a 24-inch end for sewing.

Fold last rnd toward WS of piece. With tapestry needle and A, sew through back lp of sc of last rnd and unused lp of corresponding sc 2 rows below to form casing. Leave small opening for threading elastic through casing.

## Top Casing Edging

Hold piece with RS facing you, with E hook, join A with sl st in front lp of first st of row 2 of Top Casing, *ch 2, sl st in back bar of 2nd ch from hook—*picot made*, sk next 2 sc, sl st in next sc, rep from * around, join with sl st in joining sl st.

Fasten off and weave in ends.

## Strap
### Make 2

With E hook and A, ch 29 [31, 33, 35], working in back bar only, sl st in 2nd ch from hook and in each rem ch.

Fasten off and weave in ends.

## Finishing

On top edge, place marker in centre st of both Halter Back and Front. Place markers 1½, [1¾, 2, 2¼] inches from centre st on Halter Front and ¾ inch from centre st on Halter Back. Sew RS of Strap ends at base of casings, left Strap on front marker and back marker, and right Strap on front marker and back marker.

Cut 2 pieces of ⅛-inch-wide elastic approximately 2–3 inches less than finished Halter circumference, or desired length for comfort. Place safety pin at end of each piece of elastic, pull through each Casing to desired tightness. Overlap ends of elastic about 1 inch, with sewing needle and matching thread, st ends securely. Sew opening closed.

## Panty Front

**Row 1:** Starting at front crotch, with G hook and B, ch 11 [12, 13, 14], working in back bar only, sc in 2nd ch from hook and in each rem ch, turn. *(10 [11, 12, 13] sc)*

**Row 2:** Ch 1, sc in each sc, turn.

**Rows 3–8:** Rep row 2.

**Row 9:** Ch 1, 2 sc in first sc, sc in each sc to last sc, 2 sc in last sc, turn. *(12 [13, 14, 15] sc)*

**Row 10:** Rep row 2.

**Rows 11 & 12 [11–14, 11–14, 11–16]:** [Work rows 9 and 10] 1 [2, 2, 3] time(s). *(14 [17, 18, 21] sc at end of last row)*

**Row 13 [15, 15, 17]:** Ch 5 [6, 7, 7], sc in 2nd ch from hook, in next 3 [4, 5, 5] chs, and in each sc, turn. *(18 [22, 24, 27] sc)*

**Row 14 [16, 16, 18]:** Ch 5 [6, 7, 7], sc in 2nd ch from hook, in next 3 [4, 5, 5] chs, and in each sc, turn. *(22 [27, 30, 33] sc)*

**Rows 15–24 [17–26, 17–28, 19–30]:** Rep row 2.

**Row 25 [27, 29, 31]:** Ch 1, sc dec, in first 2 sc, sc in each sc to last 2 sc, sc dec in last 2 sc. *(20 [25, 28, 31] sc)*

Fasten off and weave in ends.

## Panty Back

**Row 1:** Starting at back crotch, with G hook and B, ch 11 [12, 13, 14], working in back bar only, sc in 2nd ch from hook and in each rem ch, turn. *(10 [11, 12, 13] sc)*

**Row 2:** Ch 1, sc in each sc, turn.

**Row 3:** Ch 1, 2 sc in first sc, sc in next 8 [9, 10, 11] sc, 2 sc in last sc, turn. *(12 [13, 14, 15] sc)*

**Row 4:** Rep row 2.

**Row 5:** Ch 1, 2 sc in first sc, sc in each sc to last sc, 2 sc in last sc, turn. *(14 [15, 16, 17] sc)*

**Rows 6–11 [6–13, 6–13, 6–15]:** [Work rows 4 and 5] 3 [4, 4, 5] times. *(20 [23, 24, 27] sc at end of last row)*

**Row 12 [14, 14, 16]:** Rep row 2.

**Row 13 [15, 15, 17]:** Ch 4, sc in 2nd ch from hook, in next 2 chs, and in each sc, turn. *(23 [26, 28, 30] sc)*

**Row 14 [16, 16, 18]:** Ch 4, sc in 2nd ch from hook, in next 2 chs, and in each sc, turn. *(26 [29, 31, 33] sc)*

**Rows 15–24 [17–26, 17–28, 19–30]:** Rep row 2.

**Row 25 [27, 29, 31]:** Ch 1, sc dec in first 2 sc, sc in each sc to last sc, sc dec.

Fasten off and weave in ends.

## Assembly

Holding pieces with RS tog, with tapestry needle and B, sew side and crotch seams.

## Waistband

**Rnd 1 (RS):** With G hook, join A with sl st in front lp of centre sc of Panty Back, ch 1, sc in same lp, working in front lps only, sc in each sc, join with sl st in first sc.

**Rnd 2:** Ch 1, sc in same sc and in each rem sc, join with sl st in first sc.

**Rnd 3:** Ch 1, sc in same sc and in each rem sc, join with sl st in back lp of first sc.

**Rnd 4:** Ch 1, sc in same lp and in back lp of each rem sc, join with sl st in first sc.

**Rnds 5–6:** Rep rnd 2.

Fasten off, leaving a 24-inch end for sewing. Weave in rem end.

## Finishing

Fold Waistband in half. On WS, with tapestry needle and long end, sew edge to unused lps of rnd 1, forming casing.

Cut piece of ½-inch-wide elastic approximately 4 inches less than waist size. Place safety pin at end of elastic, pull through casing to desired tightness. With sewing needle and matching thread, overlap elastic ends 1 inch and sew to secure. Sew opening of Waistband closed.

## Leg Edging

Hold piece with RS facing you, with G hook, join A with sl st in first st to left of crotch seam, *ch 2, sl st in back bar of 2nd ch from hook—*picot made,* sk next 2 sc rows, sl st in end of next sc row, rep from * around, join with sl st in joining sl st.

Fasten off and weave in all ends.

Rep on rem Leg.

# Poncho

## Panel
**Make 2**

**Row 1:** With G hook and A, ch 57 [60, 63], sc in 2nd ch from hook and in each rem sc, turn. *(56 [59, 62] sc)*

**Row 2 (RS):** Ch 3 *(counts as a dc on this and following rows)*, *sk next sc, dc in next 2 sc, working around last 2 dc made, dc in sk sc, rep from * to last sc, dc in last sc, turn.

**Row 3:** Ch 1, sc in each st, turn. *(56 [59, 62] sc)*

Rep rows 2 and 3 until piece measures 5¾ [6½, 7¼] inches from beg.

## Edging
Ch 1, 3 sc in first sc, sc in each sc to last sc, 3 sc in last sc, working across next side in sps formed by edge dc and turning chs, *ch 1, 2 sc in end of next dc row, sk next sc row, rep from * to next corner, working across next side in unused lps of beg ch, 3 sc in first lp, sc in each lp to last lp, 3 sc in last lp, working across next side in sps formed by edge dc and turning chs, **ch 1, 2 sc in end of next dc row, sk next sc row, rep from ** to first sc, ch 1, join with sl st in first sc.

Fasten off and weave in all ends.

## Assembly

Referring to Assembly Diagram and with tapestry needle and A, sew Panels tog.

## Daisy

**Rnd 1 (RS):** With size 5 hook and D, ch 5, join with sl st to form a ring, ch 1, 8 sc in ring. Fasten off.

**Rnd 2:** With size 5 hook, join C with sl st in any sc, ch 3, in same sc work (tr, ch 3, sl st)—*petal made*, in each rem sc work (sl st, ch 3, tr, sl st)—*petal made*, join with sl st in joining sl st.

Fasten off and weave in all ends.

## Finishing

Referring to photo for placement, sew Daisy to centre front of Poncho. ■

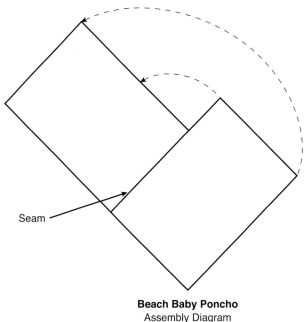

Seam

**Beach Baby Poncho**
Assembly Diagram

# PRETTY IN PINK SWEATER

*This quick-to-make sweater will keep your little princess warm and toasty.*

Design | Catherine Costa

## Skill Level
**EASY**

## Sizes
Instructions given fit size 6 months; changes for sizes 12 months and 18 months are in [ ].

## Finished Measurements
Chest: 19 [20, 21½] inches

## Materials
DK weight yarn (431 yds/160g per ball):
   2 balls pink, 1 ball blue
Size J/10/6mm crochet hook or size needed
   to obtain gauge
Tapestry needle
Stitch markers
3 (15mm) buttons

**3**
**LIGHT**

## Gauge
**With 2 strands of yarn held tog:** 5 sc = 2 inches;
   5 rows = 1½ inches
Take time to check gauge.

## Notes
Weave in loose ends as work progresses.

Join rounds with a slip stitch unless otherwise stated.

## Back
**Row 1:** Starting at bottom edge with 2 strands of pink held tog, ch 26 [29, 31] sc in 2nd ch from hook, sc in each rem ch across, turn. *(25 [28, 30] sc)*

**Row 2:** Ch 1, sc in each sc across, turn.

Rep row 2 until Back measures 6½ [7, 7½] inches from beg. For **underarm**, place st marker at each edge.

Rep row 2 until Back measures 9½ [10¾, 11½] inches from beg.

### Left Shoulder Shaping
**Row 1:** Ch 1, sc in each of next 9 [10, 11] sc, turn.

**Row 2:** Ch 1, sc in each sc across, turn.

Rep row 2 until Left Shoulder measures 1½ inches, fasten off.

### Right Shoulder Shaping
**Row 1:** With finished Left Shoulder to the right, sk next 7 [8, 8] sc of last row of Back, attach 2 strands of pink in next sc, ch 1, sc in same sc as beg ch-1, sc in each of next 8 [9, 10] sc, turn. *(9 [10, 11] sc)*

**Row 2:** Ch 1, sc in each sc across, turn.

Rep row 2 until Right Shoulder measures 1½ inches, fasten off.

## Front

**Row 1:** Starting at bottom edge with 2 strands of pink, ch 26 [29, 31] sc in 2nd ch from hook, sc in each rem ch across, turn. *(25 [28, 30] sc)*

**Row 2:** Ch 1, sc in each sc across, turn.

Rep row 2 until Front from beg measures 6½ [7, 7½] inches. For underarm, place st marker at each edge.

Rep row 2 until Front from beg measures 7½ [8½, 9] inches.

### Left Neck & Shoulder Shaping

**Row 1:** Ch 1, sc in each of next 9 [10, 11] sc, turn.

**Row 2:** Ch 1, sc in each sc across, turn.

Rep row 2 until Left Neck & Shoulder Shaping measures 3½ [3¾, 4] inches, then work 1 extra row of buttonhole row as follows:

**Buttonhole row:** Ch 1, sc in 1 [2, 2] sc, ch 1, sk next sc, [sc in each of next 2 sc, ch 1, sk next sc] twice, sc in next 1 [1, 2] sc st(s), turn. *(3 buttonholes)*

**Next row:** Ch 1, sc in each st across, fasten off.

### Right Shoulder Shaping

**Row 1:** With finished Left Shoulder to the right, sk next 7 [8, 8] sc of last row of Front, attach 2 strands of pink in next sc, ch 1, sc in same sc as beg ch-1, sc in each of next 8 [9, 10] sc, turn. *(9 [10, 11] sc)*

**Row 2:** Ch 1, sc in each sc across, turn.

Rep row 2 until Right Shoulder measures 3½ [3¾, 4] inches, fasten off.

## Sleeve

**Make 2**

**Row 1:** Starting at wrist area of Sleeve, with 2 strands of pink, ch 18 [19, 21], sc in 2nd ch from hook, sc in each rem ch across, turn. *(17 [18, 20] sc)*

**Row 2:** Ch 1, sc in each sc across, turn.

**Row 3:** Ch 1, 2 sc in first sc, sc in each rem sc across, turn.

**Next rows:** [Rep rows 2 and 3 alternately] 4 [7, 7] times. *(22 [26, 28] sc)*

Rep row 2 until total length of Sleeve is 6½ [7¼, 8] inches, fasten off.

## Finishing

With RS facing, whipstitch right shoulder closed.

Position buttons on Back Left Shoulder and sew in place opposite buttonholes. Button shoulder buttons and tack ends of overlapped rows of button and buttonhole placket.

Sew sleeves into armhole openings, sew sleeve and side seams.

## Neckline Trim

Attach 2 strands pink at right shoulder seam, ch 1, sc evenly spaced around Neckline opening, join in beg sc, fasten off.

## Top Stitching

Working between rows 1 and 2 of Sweater bottom edge, holding 2 strands of blue tog on WS of Sweater at seam and leaving a 2-inch length, beg on RS, insert hook RS to WS, draw up a lp of yarn and draw through from WS to RS, [insert hook RS to WS in next st to the right, yo, draw up a

lp from WS to RS, draw through lp on hook] around bottom edge of Sweater, ending with last st in same st as beg st, leaving a 2-inch length, fasten off. With all ends on WS, knot ends tog, weave ends in on underside of ch, fasten off rem pieces.

Rep Top Stitching between rows 1 and 2 of each Sleeve. ■

# WHITE RUFFLED BABY DRESS

*When adorned in this frilly gown, your little angel will capture everyone's heart.*

Design | Robin L. Murphy

## Skill Level

**EASY**

## Finished Sizes

Instructions given are for 3–6 months; changes for 6–9 months and 9–12 months are in [ ].

## Materials

Sport weight yarn (250 yds/160g per ball):

**3**
**LIGHT**

    4 [5, 6] balls white

4 white ⅜-inch buttons

2 flower-shaped ⅞-inch buttons

Tapestry needle

Size E/4/3.5mm crochet hook or size needed to obtain gauge

## Gauge

5 sc = 1 inch; 6 sc back lp rows = 1 inch; 4 shell rows = 2¼ inches

Take time to check gauge.

## Special Stitches

**Beginning V-stitch (beg V-st):** Ch 5, dc in same st.

**V-stitch (V-st):** (Dc, ch 2, dc) in next st.

## Bodice

**Row 1:** Ch 56, sc in 2nd ch from hook, sc in next 5 chs, 3 sc in next ch, *sc in next 13 chs, 3 sc in next ch, rep from * 2 more times, sc in last 6 chs, turn. *(63 sc)*

*Note: Work the following rows in back lps only, unless otherwise stated.*

**Rows 2–11 [2–12, 2–13]:** Ch 1, sc in each st across with 3 sc in each centre corner st, turn, ending with 143 [151, 159] sc in last row.

**Row 12 [13, 14]:** Ch 1, sc in first 18 [19, 20] sts, for **first armhole**, ch 9, sk next 35 [37, 39] sts, sc in next 37 [39, 41] sts, for **2nd armhole**, ch 9, sk next 35 [37, 39] sts, sc in last 18 [19, 20] sts, turn. *(73 sc, 2 ch-9 sps [77 sc, 2 ch-9 sps; 81 sc, 2 ch-9 sps])*

**Row 13 [14, 15]:** Ch 1, sc in each st and in each ch across, turn. *(91 sc [95 sc, 99 sc])*

**Rows 14—19 [15—21, 16—25]:** Ch 1, sc in each st across. At end of last row, fasten off.

### White Ruffled Baby Dress
Sample project was crocheted with Red Heart
Sport (100 per cent acrylic) from Coats & Clark.

## Buttonhole Placket

**Row 1:** Working in ends of rows across left back, with RS of work facing you, join with sc in first row, sc in each row across, turn. *(19 sc [21 sc, 25 sc])*

**Row 2:** Ch 1, sc in each st across, turn.

**Row 3:** Ch 1, sc in first 4 [4, 6] sts, for **buttonhole**, ch 2, sk next 2 sts, *sc in next 4 [5, 6] sts, for **buttonhole**, ch 2, sk next 2 sts, rep from * 1 more time, sc in last st, turn.

**Row 4:** Ch 1, sc in each st and 2 sc in each ch-2 sp across, turn. *(19 sc [21 sc, 25 sc])*

**Row 5:** Ch 1, sc in each st across, fasten off.

## Button Placket

**Row 1:** Working in ends of rows across right back, with RS of work facing you, join with sc in first row, sc in each row across, turn. *(19 sc [21 sc, 25 sc])*

**Rows 2—5:** Ch 1, sc in each st across, turn. At end of last row, fasten off.

## Neck Trim

Working in ends of rows across Button and Buttonhole Plackets and in starting ch on opposite side of row 1 on Bodice, with RS of work facing you, join with sc in last row on Button Placket, working from left to right, reverse sc in each row and in each ch across, fasten off.

## Skirt

**Rnd 1:** Working in ends of rows of Button and Buttonhole Plackets and on last row of Bodice, hold Buttonhole Placket over Button Placket, matching rows and working through both thicknesses, join with sc in first row, sc in next 4 rows, working on Bodice only, sc in each st around, join with sl st in first sc. *(96 sc [100 sc, 104 sc])*

**Rnd 2:** Beg V-st *(see Special Stitches on page 46)*, sk next st, [V-st *(see Special Stitches on page 46)* in next st, sk next st] around, join with sl st in 3rd ch of ch-5. *(48 V-sts [50 V-sts, 52 V-sts])*

**Rnd 3:** Sl st in next ch sp, ch 3, (dc, ch 2, 2 dc) in same sp, (2 dc, ch 2, 2 dc) in ch sp of each V-st around, join with sl st in top of ch-3.

**Rnds 4 & 5 [4–6, 4–7]:** Sl st in next st, sl st in next ch sp, ch 3, (dc, ch 2, 2 dc) in same sp, (2 dc, ch 2, 2 dc) in each ch sp around, join.

**Rnd 6 [7, 8]:** Sl st in next st, sl st in next ch sp, ch 3, (2 dc, ch 2, 3 dc) in same sp, (3 dc, ch 2, 3 dc) in each ch sp around, join.

**Rnds 7—12 [8—14, 9—16]:** Sl st in each of next 2 sts, sl st in next ch sp, ch 3, (2 dc, ch 2, 3 dc) in same sp, (3 dc, ch 2, 3 dc) in each ch sp around, join.

**Rnd 13 [15, 17]:** Sl st in each of next 2 sts, sl st in next ch sp, ch 3, 7 dc in same sp, for scallop, 8 dc in each ch sp around, join.

**Rnd 14 [16, 18]:** Sl st in next 4 sts, 9 dc in sp between last scallop and next scallop, [sl st in 5th dc of next scallop, 9 dc in sp between last scallop and next scallop] around, join with sl st in first sl st, fasten off.

## Sleeve

**Rnd 1:** Working around armhole, join with sl st in 5th ch at underarm, beg V-st, [sk next ch, V-st in next ch] 2 times, V-st in next st, [sk next st, V-st in next st] 17 [18, 19] times, [V-st in next ch, sk next ch] 2 times, join with sl st in 3rd ch of ch-5. *(23 V-sts [24 V-sts, 25 V-sts])*

**Rnd 2:** Rep rnd 3 of Skirt.

**Rnds 3 & 4 [3–5, 3–6]:** Rep rnd 4 of Skirt.

**Rnd 5 [6, 7]:** Sl st in next st, sl st in next ch sp, ch 1, sc in same sp, sc in each ch sp around, join with sl st in first sc. *(23 sc [24 sc, 25 sc])*

**Rnds 6–8 [7–9, 8–10]:** Ch 1, sc in each st around, join. At end of last rnd, fasten off.

Rep on other armhole.

## Finishing

Sew white buttons to Button Placket opposite buttonholes.

Sew flower-shaped buttons to centre front of Bodice as shown in photo. ∎

# LITTLE BOY BLUE

*This cozy winter wear is easy to stitch and will look great on your little guy.*

Design | Laura Gebhardt

## Skill Level

**EASY**

## Sizes

Instructions given fit size 6 months; changes for 12 months, 18 months and 24 months are in [ ].

## Finished Measurements

Chest: 19 [20, 21, 22½] inches
Hat: 14 [14, 16, 16] inches in circumference

## Materials

DK weight yarn (575 yds/198g per skein):
  1 [2, 2, 2] skein(s) powder blue
Size G/6/4mm crochet hook or size needed to obtain gauge
Tapestry needle
4 blue shank buttons:
    ⅜ inch for sizes 6 and 12 months
    ½ inch for sizes 18 and 24 months

## Gauge

18 hdc = 4 inches
Take time to check gauge.

## Special Stitches

**Front post double crochet (fpdc):** Yo, insert hook from front to back to front around **post** *(see Stitch Guide on page 126)* of st indicated, draw lp through, [yo, draw through 2 lps on hook] twice.

**Back post double crochet (bpdc):** Yo, insert hook from back to front to back around **post** *(see Stitch Guide on page 126)* of st indicated, draw lp through, [yo, draw through 2 lps on hook] twice.

# Sweater

## Back

**Row 1 (RS):** Ch 44 [46, 48, 52], hdc in 3rd ch from hook *(beg 2 sk chs count as a hdc)* and in each rem ch, turn. *(43 [45, 47, 51] hdc)*

**Row 2:** Ch 2, *hdc in **back lp** *(see Stitch Guide on page 126)* of next hdc, hdc in **front lp** *(see Stitch Guide on page 126)* of next hdc, rep from * to last hdc and beg 2 sk chs, hdc in back lp of last hdc and in 2nd ch of beg 2 sk chs, turn.

**Row 3:** Ch 2, *hdc in back lp of next hdc, hdc in front lp of next hdc, rep from * to last hdc and turning ch-2, hdc in back lp of next hdc and in 2nd ch of turning ch-2, turn.

**Rows 4–22 [4–24, 4–26, 4–28]:** Rep row 3.

Fasten off and weave in ends.

## Left Front

**Row 1 (RS):** Ch 28 [30, 30, 32], hdc in 3rd ch from hook *(beg 2 sk chs count as a hdc)* and in each rem ch, turn. *(27 [29, 29, 31] hdc)*

Little Boy Blue
Sample projects were crocheted
with Red Heart Soft Baby (100 per
cent acrylic) from Coats & Clark.

**Row 2:** Ch 2, *hdc in back lp of next hdc, hdc in front lp of next hdc, rep from * to last hdc and beg 2 sk chs, hdc in back lp of last hdc and in 2nd ch of beg 2 sk chs, turn.

**Row 3:** Ch 2, *hdc in back lp of next hdc, hdc in front lp of next hdc, rep from * to last hdc and turning ch-2, hdc in back lp of next hdc and in 2nd ch of turning ch-2, turn.

**Row 4:** Rep row 3.

**Row 5:** Ch 2, *hdc in back lp of next hdc, hdc in front lp of next hdc, rep from * 8 [9, 9, 10] times, ch 1—*buttonhole made*, sk next hdc, [hdc in front lp of next hdc, hdc in back lp of next hdc] twice, ch 1—*buttonhole made*, sk next hdc, hdc in back lp of next hdc and in 2nd ch of turning ch-2, turn.

**Row 6:** Ch 2, hdc in back lp of next hdc and in next ch, [hdc in back lp of next hdc, hdc in front lp of next hdc] twice, hdc in next ch and in front lp of next hdc, *hdc in back lp of next hdc, hdc in front lp of next hdc, rep from * to last hdc and turning ch-2, hdc in back lp of last hdc and in 2nd ch of turning ch-2.

**Rows 7 & 8 [7 & 8, 7–10, 7–10]:** Rep row 3.

**Rows 9 & 10 [9 & 10, 11 & 12, 11 & 12]:** Rep rows 5 and 6.

**Row 11 [11, 13, 13]:** Ch 2, *hdc in back lp of next hdc, hdc in front lp of next hdc, rep from * to last hdc and turning ch-2, **hdc dec** *(see Stitch Guide on page 126)* in last hdc and in 2nd ch of turning ch-2, turn. *(26 [28, 28, 30] hdc)*

**Row 12 [12, 14, 14]:** Ch 1, hdc in front lp of next hdc, *hdc in back lp of next hdc, hdc in front lp of next hdc, rep from * to last hdc and turning ch-2, hdc in back lp of last hdc and in 2nd ch of turning ch-2, turn. *(25 [27, 27, 29] hdc)*

**Rows 13–22 [13–24, 15–26, 15–26]:** [Work last 2 rows] 5 [6, 6, 6] times. *(15 [15, 15, 17] hdc at end of last row)*

### For Sizes 6, 12 & 18 Months Only
Fasten off and weave in ends.

Continue with Right Front.

### For Size 24 Months Only
**Rows 27 & 28:** Rep row 3.

Fasten off and weave in ends.

Continue with Right Front.

## Right Front
**Row 1 (RS):** Ch 28 [30, 30, 32], hdc in 3rd ch from hook *(beg 2 sk chs count as a hdc)* and in each rem ch, turn. *(27 [29, 29, 31] hdc)*

**Row 2:** Ch 2, *hdc in back lp of next hdc, hdc in front lp of next hdc, rep from * to last hdc and beg 2 sk chs, hdc in back lp of last hdc and in 2nd ch of beg 2 sk chs, turn.

**Row 3:** Ch 2, *hdc in back lp of next hdc, hdc in front lp of next hdc, rep from * to last hdc and turning ch-2, hdc in back lp of next hdc and in 2nd ch of turning ch-2, turn.

**Rows 4–10 [4–10, 4–12, 4–12]:** Rep row 3.

**Row 11 [11, 13, 13]:** Ch 1, *hdc in back lp of next hdc, hdc in front lp of next hdc, rep from * to last hdc and turning ch-2, hdc in back lp of next hdc and in 2nd ch of turning ch-2, turn. *(26 [28, 28, 30] hdc)*

**Row 12 [12, 14, 14]:** Ch 2, *hdc in back lp of next hdc, hdc in front lp of next hdc, rep from * to last 3 hdc, hdc in back lp of next hdc, hdc dec in last 2 hdc, turn. *(25 [27, 27, 29] hdc)*

**Rows 13–22 [13–24, 15–26, 15–26]:** [Work last 2 rows] 5 [6, 6, 6] times. *(15 [15, 15, 17] hdc at end of last row)*

## For Sizes 6, 12 & 18 Months Only
Fasten off and weave in ends.

Continue with Sleeve.

## For Size 24 Months Only
**Rows 27 & 28:** Rep row 3.

Fasten off and weave in ends.

Continue with Sleeve.

## Sleeve
Make 2

**Row 1:** Ch 24 [24, 28, 28], hdc in 3rd ch from hook *(beg 2 sk chs count as a hdc)* and in each rem ch, turn. *(23 [23, 27, 27] hdc)*

**Row 2:** Ch 2, *hdc in back lp of next hdc, hdc in front lp of next hdc, rep from * to last hdc and beg 2 sk chs, hdc in back lp of last hdc and in 2nd ch of beg 2 sk chs, turn.

**Row 3:** Ch 2, hdc in first hdc, *hdc in back lp of next hdc, hdc in front lp of next hdc, rep from * to last hdc and turning ch-2, hdc in back lp of next hdc, 2 hdc in 2nd ch of turning ch-2, turn. *(25 [25, 29, 29] hdc)*

**Row 4:** Ch 2, hdc in front lp of next hdc, *hdc in back lp of next hdc, hdc in front lp of next hdc, rep from * to turning ch-2, hdc in 2nd ch of turning ch-2, turn.

**Row 5:** Ch 2, hdc in first hdc and in front lp of next hdc, *hdc in back lp of next hdc, hdc in front lp of next hdc, rep from * to turning ch-2, 2 hdc in 2nd ch of turning ch-2, turn. *(27 [27, 29, 29] hdc)*

**Row 6:** Ch 2, *hdc in back lp of next hdc, hdc in front lp of next hdc, rep from * to last hdc and turning ch-2, hdc in back lp of last hdc, hdc in 2nd ch of turning ch-2, turn.

**Row 7:** Ch 2, hdc in first hdc, *hdc in back lp of next hdc, hdc in front lp of next hdc, rep from * to last hdc and turning ch-2, hdc in back lp of last hdc, 2 hdc in 2nd ch of turning ch-2, turn. *(29 [29, 33, 33] hdc)*

**Row 8:** Ch 2, hdc in front lp of next hdc, *hdc in back lp of next hdc, hdc in front lp of next hdc, rep from * to turning ch-2, hdc in 2nd ch of turning ch-2, turn.

**Row 9:** Ch 2, hdc in first hdc and in front lp of next hdc, *hdc in back lp of next hdc, hdc in front lp of next hdc, rep from * to turning ch-2, 2 hdc in 2nd ch of turning ch-2, turn. *(31 [31, 35, 35] hdc)*

**Row 10:** Ch 2, *hdc in back lp of next hdc, hdc in front lp of next hdc, rep from * to last hdc and turning ch-2, hdc in back lp of last hdc and in 2nd ch of turning ch-2, turn.

**Row 11:** Ch 2, hdc in first hdc, *hdc in back lp of next hdc, hdc in front lp of next hdc, rep from * to last hdc and turning ch-2, hdc in back lp of last hdc, 2 hdc in 2nd ch of turning ch-2, turn. *(33 [33, 37, 37] hdc)*

## For Sizes 6 & 12 Months Only
**Row 12:** Ch 2, hdc in front lp of next hdc, *hdc in back lp of next hdc, hdc in front lp of next hdc, rep from * to turning ch-2, hdc in 2nd ch of turning ch-2, turn.

**Row 13:** Ch 2, hdc in first hdc and in front lp of next hdc, *hdc in back lp of next hdc, hdc in front lp of next hdc, rep from * to turning ch-2, 2 hdc in 2nd ch of turning ch-2, turn. *(35 hdc)*

**Row 14:** Ch 2, *hdc in back lp of next hdc, hdc in front lp of next hdc, rep from * to last hdc and turning ch-2, hdc in back lp of last hdc and in 2nd ch of turning ch-2, turn.

**Rows 15 & 16:** Rep row 14.

**Row 17:** Ch 2, hdc in first hdc, *hdc in back lp of next hdc, hdc in front lp of next hdc, rep from * to last hdc and turning ch-2, hdc in back lp of last hdc, 2 hdc in 2nd ch of turning ch-2, turn. *(37 hdc)*

### For Size 6 Months Only

**Row 18:** Ch 2, hdc in front lp of next hdc, *hdc in back lp of next hdc, hdc in front lp of next hdc, rep from * to turning ch-2, hdc in 2nd ch of turning ch-2.

Fasten off and weave in ends.

Continue with Assembly.

### For Size 12 Months Only

**Row 18:** Ch 2, hdc in front lp of next hdc, *hdc in back lp of next hdc, hdc in front lp of next hdc, rep from * to turning ch-2, hdc in 2nd ch of turning ch-2.

**Rows 19–21:** Rep row 18.

Fasten off and weave in ends.

Continue with Assembly.

### For Sizes 18 & 24 Months Only

**Row 12:** Ch 2, hdc in front lp of next hdc, *hdc in back lp of next hdc, hdc in front lp of next hdc, rep from * to turning ch-2, hdc 2nd ch of turning ch-2, turn.

**Rows 13 & 14:** Rep row 12.

**Row 15:** Ch 2, hdc in first hdc and in front lp of next hdc, *hdc in back lp of next hdc, hdc in front lp of next hdc, rep from * to turning ch-2, 2 hdc in 2nd ch of turning ch-2, turn. *(39 hdc)*

**Row 16:** Ch 2, *hdc in back lp of next hdc, hdc in front lp of next hdc, rep from * to last hdc and turning ch-2, hdc in back lp of last hdc and in 2nd ch of turning ch-2, turn.

**Rows 17 & 18:** Rep row 16.

**Row 19:** Ch 2, hdc in first hdc and in front lp of next hdc, *hdc in back lp of next hdc, hdc in front lp of next hdc, rep from * to last hdc and turning ch-2, hdc in back lp of last hdc, 2 hdc in 2nd ch of turning ch-2, turn. *(41 hdc)*

**Row 20:** Ch 2, hdc in front lp of next hdc, *hdc in back lp of next hdc, hdc in front lp of next hdc, rep from * to turning ch-2, hdc in 2nd ch of turning ch-2.

**Rows 21 & 22:** Rep row 20.

### For Size 18 Months Only

Fasten off and weave in ends.

Continue with Assembly.

### For Size 24 Months Only

**Rows 23 & 24:** Rep row 20.

Fasten off and weave in ends.

Continue with Assembly.

## Assembly

Sew shoulder seams. Sew Sleeves in place and sew Sleeve and side seams.

## Sleeve Edging

**Rnd 1 (RS):** Hold 1 Sleeve with RS facing you and beg ch at top, join yarn with sl st in first unused lp of beg ch to left of seam, ch 1, sc in same lp and in each rem unused lp, join with sl st in first sc.

**Rnd 2:** Ch 1, working from left to right, work **reverse sc** (see Stitch Guide on page 126) in each sc, join with sl st in first reverse sc.

Fasten off and weave in ends.

Rep on 2nd Sleeve.

## Body & Neck Edging

**Rnd 1:** Hold piece with RS of Back facing you, join yarn in first hdc to left of right shoulder seam, ch 1, sc in same hdc and in each hdc across Back neck edge, sc evenly spaced down Left Front, across lower edge of body, up Right Front and neck edge to first sc, join with sl st in first sc.

**Rnd 2:** Ch 1, working from left to right, work reverse sc in each sc, join in first reverse sc.

Fasten off and weave in ends.

## Finishing

With sewing needle and matching thread, sew buttons on Right Front opposite buttonholes.

# Hat

**Rnd 1:** Ch 3, 8 hdc in 3rd ch from hook (beg 2 sk chs count as a hdc), join with sl st in 2nd ch of beg 2 sk chs. (9 hdc)

**Rnd 2:** Ch 2 (counts as a hdc on this and following rnds), hdc in same hdc, 2 hdc in each rem hdc, join with sl st in 2nd ch of beg ch-2. (18 hdc)

**Rnd 3:** Ch 2, hdc in each hdc, join with sl st in 2nd ch of beg ch-2.

**Rnd 4:** Ch 2, 2 hdc in next hdc, *hdc in next hdc, 2 hdc in next hdc, rep from * around, join with sl st in 2nd ch of beg ch-2. (27 hdc)

**Rnd 5:** Rep rnd 3.

**Rnd 6:** Ch 2, hdc in next hdc, 2 hdc in next hdc, *hdc in next 2 hdc, 2 hdc in next hdc, rep from * around, join with sl st in 2nd ch of beg ch-2. (36 hdc)

**Rnd 7:** Rep rnd 3.

**Rnd 8:** Ch 2, hdc in next 2 hdc, 2 hdc in next hdc, *hdc in next 3 hdc, 2 hdc in next hdc, rep from * around, join with sl st in 2nd ch of beg ch-2. (45 hdc)

**Rnds 9 & 10:** Rep rnd 3.

**Rnd 11:** Ch 2, hdc in next 3 hdc, 2 hdc in next hdc, *hdc in next 4 hdc, 2 hdc in next hdc, rep from * around, join with sl st in 2nd ch of beg ch-2. (54 hdc)

**Rnd 12:** Rep rnd 3.

**Rnd 13:** Ch 2, hdc in next 4 hdc, 2 hdc in next hdc, *hdc in next 5 hdc, 2 hdc in next hdc, rep from * around, join with sl st in 2nd ch of beg ch-2. (63 hdc)

### For Sizes 6 & 12 Months Only

**Rnds 14 & 15:** Rep rnd 3.

**Rnd 16:** Ch 2, *fpdc (see Special Stitches on page 50) around next hdc, bpdc (see Special Stitches on page 50) around next hdc, rep from * around, join with sl st in 2nd ch of beg ch-2.

**Rnd 17:** Ch 2, *fpdc around next dc, bpdc around next dc, rep from * around, join with sl st in 2nd ch of beg ch-2.

**Rnds 18–20:** Rep rnd 17.

**Rnd 21:** Ch 1, working in **front lps** *(see Stitch Guide on page 126)* only, sc in same ch as joining and in each rem st, join with sl st in first sc.

*Note: Remainder of Hat is worked in rows.*

**Row 1:** Ch 2, *hdc in back lp of next sc, hdc in front lp of next sc, rep from * to last 2 sc, hdc in **back lp** *(see Stitch Guide on page 126)* of next sc and through both lps of last sc, turn.

**Row 2:** Ch 2, *hdc in back lp of next hdc, hdc in front lp of next hdc, rep from * to last hdc and turning ch-2, hdc in back lp of next hdc and in 2nd ch of turning ch-2, turn.

**Rows 3–6:** Rep row 2.

**Row 7:** Ch 1, working left to right, work **reverse sc** *(see Stitch Guide on page 126)* in each hdc and in 2nd ch of turning ch-2.

Fasten off, leaving an 8-inch end for sewing.

Continue with Finishing.

## For Sizes 18 & 24 Months Only
**Rnd 14:** Rep rnd 3.

**Rnd 15:** Ch 2, hdc in next 5 hdc, 2 hdc in next hdc, *hdc in next 6 hdc, 2 hdc in next hdc, rep from * around, join with sl st in 2nd ch of beg ch-2. *(72 hdc)*

**Rnds 16–18:** Rep rnd 3.

**Rnd 19:** Ch 2, *fpdc *(see Special Stitches on page 50)* around next hdc, **bpdc** *(see Special Stitches on page 50)* around next hdc, rep from * around, join with sl st in 2nd ch of beg ch-2.

**Rnd 20:** Ch 2, *fpdc around next dc, bpdc around next dc, rep from * around, join with sl st in 2nd ch of beg ch-2.

**Rnds 21–24:** Rep rnd 20.

**Rnd 25:** Ch 1, working in **front lps** *(see Stitch Guide on page 126)* only, sc in same ch as joining and in each rem st, join with sl st in first sc.

*Note: Remainder of Hat is worked in rows.*

**Row 1:** Ch 2, *hdc in **back lp** *(see Stitch Guide on page 126)* of next sc, hdc in front lp of next sc, rep from * to last 2 sc, hdc in back lp of next sc and through both lps of last sc, turn.

**Row 2:** Ch 2, *hdc in back lp of next hdc, hdc in front lp of next hdc, rep from * to last hdc and turning ch-2, hdc in back lp of next hdc and in 2nd ch of turning ch-2, turn.

**Rows 3–8:** Rep row 2.

**Row 9:** Ch 1, working left to right, work **reverse sc** *(see Stitch Guide on page 126)* in each hdc and in 2nd ch of turning ch-2.

Fasten off, leaving an 8-inch end for sewing.

Continue with Finishing.

## Finishing
With tapestry needle and long end, sew back seam of Hat cuff. Fold cuff up at rnd 21 [21, 25, 25]. ■

# SEASIDE CARDIGAN

*Your little one will be quite snug in this handsome cardigan.*

Design | Nanette Seale

## Skill Level

EASY

## Sizes

Instructions given fit size 6 months; changes for 12 months, 18 months and 24 months are in [ ].

## Finished Measurements

**Chest:** 19 [20, 21, 22½] inches

## Materials

DK weight yarn (455 yds/140g per ball):
  1 [2, 2, 2] ball(s) baby denim marl (A),
  1 ball pale blue (B)

Size 10 crochet cotton thread: small amount light blue (C),
  small amount dark blue (D)
Size I/9/5.5mm crochet hook or size needed to obtain
  gauge
Size 7/1.65mm steel crochet hook (for fish)
Tapestry needle
6 white ⅝-inch buttons
Sewing needle and matching thread

## Gauge

**Size I hook:** 16 sc = 4 inches
Take time to check gauge.

## Body

**Row 1 (WS):** With size I hook and A, ch 77 [81, 85, 89], working in **front lps** (*see Stitch Guide on page 126*) only,

sc in 2nd ch from hook and in each rem ch, turn. (*76 [80, 84, 88] sc*)

**Row 2 (RS):** Ch 1, sc in first unused lp of beg ch and in front lp of first sc at same time, *sc in next unused lp of beg ch and in front lp of next sc at same time, rep from * across, turn.

**Row 3:** Ch 1, sc in first unused lp on 2nd row below and in front lp of first sc at same time, *sc in next unused lp on 2nd row below and in front lp of next sc at same time, rep from * across, turn.

**Rows 4–47 [4–51, 4–55, 4–59]:** Rep row 3.

### Right Front

**Row 48 [52, 56, 60]:** Ch 1, sc in first unused lp on 2nd row below and in front lp of first sc at same time, *sc in next unused lp on 2nd row below and in front lp of next sc at same time, rep from * 14 [15, 16, 17] times, turn, leaving rem sc unworked. (*16 [17, 18, 19] sc*)

**Rows 49–59 [53–63, 57–69, 61–79]:** Rep row 3.

### Neck Shaping

*Note: On following rows, work sc dec through unused lp indicated on 2nd row below and front lps of sc indicated on working row.*

**Row 60 [64, 70, 80]:** Ch 1, **sc dec** (*see Stitch Guide on page 126*) in first 2 sc, *sc in next unused lp on 2nd row below and in front lp of next sc at same time, rep from * across, turn. *(15 [16, 17, 18] sc)*

**Row 61 [65, 71, 81]:** Rep row 3.

**Row 62 [66, 72, 82]:** Ch 1, sc dec in first 2 sc, *sc in next unused lp on 2nd row below and in front lp of next sc at same time, rep from * across, turn. *(14 [15, 16, 17] sc)*

## For Size 6 Months Only

**Row 63:** Ch 1, sc in first unused lp on 2nd row below and in front lp of first sc at same time, *sc in next unused lp on 2nd row below and in front lp of next sc at same time, rep from * to last 2 sc, sc dec, turn. *(13 sc)*

**Row 64:** Ch 1, sc dec in first 2 sc, *sc in next unused lp on 2nd row below and in front lp of next sc at same time, rep from * across, turn. *(12 sc)*

**Row 65:** Ch 1, sc in first unused lp on 2nd row below and in front lp of first sc at same time, *sc in next unused lp on 2nd row below and in front lp of next sc at same time, rep from * 7 times, turn, leaving rem sc unworked. *(9 sc)*

**Row 66:** Ch 1, sc in first unused lp on 2nd row below and through both lps of first sc at same time, *sc in next unused lp on 2nd row below and through both lps of next sc at same time, rep from * across.

Fasten off and weave in ends.

Continue with Back.

## For Sizes 12, 18 & 24 Months Only

**Row 67 [73, 83]:** Rep row 3.

**Row 68 [74, 84]:** Ch 1, sc dec in first 2 sc, *sc in next unused lp on 2nd row below and in front lp of next sc at same time, rep from * across, turn. *(14 [15, 16] sc)*

**Row 69 [75, 85]:** Rep row 3.

**Row 70 [76, 86]:** Ch 1, sc dec in first 2 sc, *sc in next unused lp on 2nd row below and in front lp of next sc at same time, rep from * across, turn. *(13 [14, 15] sc)*

## For Size 12 Months Only

**Row 71:** Ch 1, sc in first unused lp on 2nd row below and in front lp of first sc at same time, *sc in next unused lp on 2nd row below and in front lp of next sc at same time, rep from * 8 times, turn, leaving rem sc unworked. *(10 sc)*

**Row 72:** Ch 1, sc in first unused lp on 2nd row below and through both lps of first sc at same time, *sc in next unused lp on 2nd row below and through both lps of next sc at same time, rep from * across.

Fasten off and weave in ends.

Continue with Back.

## For Sizes 18 & 24 Months Only

**Row 77 [87]:** Rep row 3.

**Row 78 [88]:** Ch 1, sc dec in first 2 sc, *sc in next unused lp on 2nd row below and in front lp of next sc at same time, rep from * across, turn. *(13 [14] sc)*

## For Size 18 Months Only

**Row 79:** Ch 1, sc in first unused lp on 2nd row below and in front lp of first sc at same time, *sc in next unused lp on 2nd row below and in front lp of next sc at same time, rep from * 8 times, turn, leaving rem sc unworked. *(10 sc)*

**Row 80:** Ch 1, sc in first unused lp on 2nd row below and through both lps of first sc at same time, *sc in next unused lp on 2nd row below and through both lps of next sc at same time, rep from * across.

Fasten off and weave in ends.

Continue with Back.

### Seaside Cardigan

Sample project was crocheted with Softee Baby (100 per cent acrylic) from Bernat and Aunt Lydia's Classic Crochet Thread (100 per cent mercerized cotton) from Coats & Clark.

## For Size 24 Months Only

**Row 89:** Rep row 3.

**Row 90:** Sl st in first 2 sc, ch 1, *sc in next unused lp on 2nd row below and in front lp of next sc at same time, rep from * 11 times, turn. *(12 sc)*

**Row 91:** Ch 1, sc in first unused lp on 2nd row below and through both lps of first sc at same time, *sc in next unused lp on 2nd row below and through both lps of next sc at same time, rep from * across.

Fasten off and weave in ends.

Continue with Back.

## Back

**Row 48 [52, 56, 60]:** Holding piece with RS facing you, sk next 4 sc on row 47 [51, 55, 59] from Right Front, join A with sl st in front lp of next sc, ch 1, sc in corresponding unused lp on 2nd row below and in same lp as joining, *sc in next unused lp on 2nd row below and in front lp of next sc at same time, rep from * 34 [36, 38, 40] times, turn, leaving rem sc unworked. *(36 [38, 40, 42] sc)*

**Rows 49–63 [53–69, 57–77, 61–84]:** Rep row 3.

## For Size 6 Months Only

### Right Shoulder

**Row 64:** Ch 1, sc in first unused lp on 2nd row below and in front lp of first sc at same time, *sc in next unused lp on 2nd row below and in front lp of next sc at same time, rep from * 13 times, turn, leaving rem sc unworked. *(15 sc)*

**Row 65:** Ch 1, sc dec in first 2 sc, *sc in next unused lp on 2nd row below and in front lp of next sc at same time, rep from * across, turn. *(14 sc)*

**Row 66:** Ch 1, sc in first unused lp on 2nd row below and in front lp of first sc at same time, *sc in next unused lp on 2nd row below and in front lp of next sc at same time, rep from * 9 times, turn, leaving rem sc unworked. *(11 sc)*

*Note: On following row, work sc dec through corresponding unused lps on 2nd row below and both lps of sc indicated.*

**Row 67:** Ch 1, sc dec in first 2 sc, sc dec in next 2 sc, *sc in next unused lp on 2nd row below and through both lps of next sc at same time, rep from * across. *(9 sc)*

Fasten off.

### Left Shoulder

**Row 64:** Holding Back with RS facing you, sk next 6 sc on row 63 from Right Shoulder, join A with sl st in front lp of next sc, ch 1, sc in corresponding unused lp on 2nd row below and in same lp as joining, *sc in next unused lp on 2nd row below and in front lp of next sc at same time, rep from * across, turn. *(15 sc)*

**Row 65:** Ch 1, sc in first unused lp on 2nd row below and in front lp of first sc at same time, *sc in next unused lp on 2nd row below and in front lp of next sc at same time, rep from * to last 2 sc, sc dec, turn. *(14 sc)*

**Row 66:** Sl st in first 3 sc, ch 1, *sc in next unused lp on 2nd row below and in front lp of next sc at same time, rep from * 10 times, turn. *(11 sc)*

*Note: On following row, work sc dec through corresponding unused lps on 2nd row below and both lps of sc indicated.*

**Row 67:** Ch 1, sc in first unused lp on 2nd row below and through both lps of first sc at same time, *sc in next unused lp on 2nd row below and through both lps of next sc at same time, rep from * 5 times, [sc dec in next 2 sc] twice. *(9 sc)*

Fasten off and weave in ends.

Continue with Left Front.

## For Size 12 Months Only

### Right Shoulder

**Row 70:** Ch 1, sc in first unused lp on 2nd row below and in front lp of first sc at same time, *sc in next unused lp on 2nd row below and in front lp of next sc at same time, rep from * 14 times, turn, leaving rem sc unworked. *(16 sc)*

**Row 71:** Ch 1, sc dec in first 2 sc, *sc in next unused lp on 2nd row below and in front lp of next sc at same time, rep from * across, turn. *(15 sc)*

**Row 72:** Ch 1, sc in first unused lp on 2nd row below and in front lp of first sc at same time, *sc in next unused lp on 2nd row below and in front lp of next sc at same time, rep from * 10 times, turn, leaving rem sc unworked. *(12 sc)*

*Note: On following row, work sc dec through corresponding unused lps on 2nd row below and both lps of sc indicated.*

**Row 73:** Ch 1, sc dec in first 2 sc, sc dec in next 2 sc, *sc in next unused lp on 2nd row below and through both lps of next sc at same time, rep from * across. *(10 sc)*

Fasten off.

### Left Shoulder

**Row 70:** Holding Back with RS facing you, sk next 6 sc on row 69 from Right Shoulder, join A with sl st in front lp of next sc, ch 1, sc in corresponding unused lp on 2nd row below and in same lp as joining, *sc in next unused lp on 2nd row below and in front lp of next sc at same time, rep from * across, turn. *(16 sc)*

**Row 71:** Ch 1, sc in first unused lp on 2nd row below and in front lp of first sc at same time, *sc in next unused lp on 2nd row below and in front lp of next sc at same time, rep from * to last 2 sc, sc dec, turn. *(15 sc)*

**Row 72:** Sl st in first 3 sc, ch 1, *sc in next unused lp on 2nd row below and in front lp of next sc at same time, rep from * 11 times, turn. *(12 sc)*

*Note: On following row, work sc dec through corresponding unused lps on 2nd row below and both lps of sc indicated.*

**Row 73:** Ch 1, sc in first unused lp on 2nd row below and through both lps of first sc at same time, *sc in next unused lp on 2nd row below and through both lps of next sc at same time, rep from * 6 times, [sc dec in next 2 sc] twice. *(10 sc)*

Fasten off and weave in ends.

Continue with Left Front.

## For Size 18 Months Only

### Right Shoulder

**Row 78:** Ch 1, sc in first unused lp on 2nd row below and in front lp of first sc at same time, *sc in next unused lp on 2nd row below and in front lp of next sc at same time, rep from * 14 times, turn, leaving rem sc unworked.

**Row 79:** Ch 1, sc dec in first 2 sc, *sc in next unused lp on 2nd row below and in front lp of next sc at same time, rep from * across, turn. *(15 sc)*

**Row 80:** Ch 1, sc in first unused lp on 2nd row below and in front lp of first sc at same time, *sc in next unused lp on 2nd row below and in front lp of next sc at same time, rep from * 10 times, turn, leaving rem sc unworked. *(12 sc)*

*Note: On following row, work sc dec through corresponding unused lps on 2nd row below and both lps of sc indicated.*

**Row 81:** Ch 1, sc dec in first 2 sc, sc dec in next 2 sc, *sc in next unused lp on 2nd row below and through both lps of next sc at same time, rep from * across. *(10 sc)*

Fasten off.

## Left Shoulder

**Row 78:** Holding Back with RS facing you, sk next 8 sc on row 77 from Right Shoulder, join A with sl st in front lp of next sc, ch 1, sc in corresponding unused lp on 2nd row below and in same lp as joining, *sc in next unused lp on 2nd row below and in front lp of next sc at same time, rep from * across, turn. *(16 sc)*

**Row 79:** Ch 1, sc in first unused lp on 2nd row below and in front lp of first sc at same time, *sc in next unused lp on 2nd row below and in front lp of next sc at same time, rep from * to last 2 sc, sc dec, turn. *(15 sc)*

**Row 80:** Sl st in first 3 sc, ch 1, *sc in next unused lp on 2nd row below and in front lp of next sc at same time, rep from * 11 times, turn. *(12 sc)*

*Note: On following row, work sc dec through corresponding unused lps on 2nd row below and both lps of sc indicated.*

**Row 81:** Ch 1, sc in first unused lp on 2nd row below and through both lps of first sc at same time, *sc in next unused lp on 2nd row below and through both lps of next sc at same time, rep from * 6 times, [sc dec in next 2 sc] twice. *(10 sc)*

Fasten off and weave in ends.

Continue with Left Front.

## For Size 24 Months Only

### Right Shoulder

**Row 85:** Ch 1, sc in first unused lp on 2nd row below and in front lp of first sc at same time, *sc in next unused lp on 2nd row below and in front lp of next sc at same time, rep from * 15 times, turn, leaving rem sc unworked. *(17 sc)*

**Row 86:** Ch 1, sc dec in first 2 sc, *sc in next unused lp on 2nd row below and in front lp of next sc at same time, rep from * across, turn. *(16 sc)*

**Row 87:** Ch 1, sc in first unused lp on 2nd row below and in front lp of first sc at same time, *sc in next unused lp on 2nd row below and in front lp of next sc at same time, rep from * to last 2 sc, sc dec, turn. *(15 sc)*

**Row 88:** Ch 1, sc dec in first 2 sc, *sc in next unused lp on 2nd row below and in front lp of next sc at same time, rep from * across, turn. *(14 sc)*

**Row 89:** Ch 1, sc in first unused lp on 2nd row below and in front lp of first sc at same time, *sc in next unused lp on 2nd row below and in front lp of next sc at same time, rep from * to last 2 sc, sc dec, turn. *(13 sc)*

**Row 90:** Rep row 3.

**Row 91:** Ch 1, sc dec in first 2 sc, *sc in next unused lp on 2nd row below and in front lp of next sc at same time, rep from * across, turn. *(12 sc)*

**Row 92:** Ch 1, sc in first unused lp on 2nd row below and through both lps of first sc at same time, *sc in next unused lp on 2nd row below and through both lps of next sc at same time, rep from * across. Fasten off.

## Left Shoulder

**Row 85:** Holding Back with RS facing you, sk next 8 sc on row 84 from Right Shoulder, join A with sl st in front lp of next sc, ch 1, sc in corresponding unused lp on 2nd row below and in same lp as joining, *sc in next unused lp on 2nd row below and in front lp of next sc at same time, rep from * across, turn. *(17 sc)*

**Row 86:** Ch 1, sc in first unused lp on 2nd row below and in front lp of first sc at same time, *sc in next unused lp on 2nd row below and in front lp of next sc at same time, rep from * to last 2 sc, sc dec, turn. *(16 sc)*

**Row 87:** Ch 1, sc dec in first 2 sc, *sc in next unused lp on 2nd row below and in front lp of next sc at same time, rep from * across, turn. *(15 sc)*

**Row 88:** Ch 1, sc in first unused lp on 2nd row below and in front lp of first sc at same time, *sc in next unused lp on

2nd row below and in front lp of next sc at same time, rep from * to last 2 sc, sc dec, turn. *(13 sc)*

**Row 89:** Ch 1, sc dec in first 2 sc, *sc in next unused lp on 2nd row below and in front lp of next sc at same time, rep from * across, turn. *(13 sc)*

**Row 90:** Rep row 3.

**Row 91:** Ch 1, sc dec in first 2 sc, *sc in next unused lp on 2nd row below and in front lp of next sc at same time, rep from * across, turn. *(12 sc)*

**Row 92:** Ch 1, sc in first unused lp on 2nd row below and through both lps of first sc at same time, *sc in next unused lp on 2nd row below and through both lps of next sc at same time, rep from * across.

Fasten off and weave in ends.

Continue with Left Front.

## Left Front

**Row 48 [52, 56, 60]:** Holding piece with RS facing you, sk next 4 sc on row 47 [51, 55, 59] from Back, join A with sl st in front lp of next sc, ch 1, sc in corresponding unused lp on 2nd row below and in same lp as joining, *sc in next unused lp on 2nd row below and in front lp of next sc at same time, rep from * across, turn. *(16 [17, 18,19] sc)*

**Rows 49–59 [53–63, 57–69, 61–79]:** Rep row 3.

## Neck Shaping

**Row 60 [64, 70, 80]:** Ch 1, sc in first unused lp on 2nd row below and in front lp of first sc at same time, *sc in next unused lp on 2nd row below and in front lp of next sc at same time, rep from * to last 2 sc, sc dec, turn. *(15 [16, 17, 18] sc)*

**Row 61 [65, 71, 81]:** Rep row 3.

**Row 62 [66, 72, 82]:** Ch 1, sc in first unused lp on 2nd row below and in front lp of first sc at same time, *sc in next unused lp on 2nd row below and in front lp of next sc at same time, rep from * to last 2 sc, sc dec, turn. *(14 [15, 16, 17] sc)*

## For Size 6 Months Only
**Row 63:** Ch 1, sc dec in first 2 sc, *sc in next unused lp on 2nd row below and in front lp of next sc at same time, rep from * across, turn. *(13 sc)*

**Row 64:** Ch 1, sc in first unused lp on 2nd row below and in front lp of first sc at same time, *sc in next unused lp on 2nd row below and in front lp of next sc at same time, rep from * to last 2 sc, sc dec, turn. *(12 sc)*

**Row 65:** Sl st in first 3 sc, ch 1, *sc in next unused lp on 2nd row below and in front lp of next sc at same time, rep from * 8 times, turn. *(9 sc)*

**Row 66:** Ch 1, sc in first unused lp on 2nd row below and through both lps of first sc at same time, *sc in next unused lp on 2nd row below and through both lps of next sc at same time, rep from * across.

Fasten off and weave in ends.

Continue with Assembly.

## For Sizes 12, 18 & 24 Months Only
**Row 67 [73, 83]:** Rep row 3.

**Row 68 [74, 84]:** Ch 1, sc in first unused lp on 2nd row below and in front lp of first sc at same time, *sc in next unused lp on 2nd row below and in front lp of next sc at same time, rep from * to last 2 sc, sc dec, turn. *(14 [15, 16] sc)*

**Row 69 [75, 85]:** Rep row 3.

**Row 70 [76, 86]:** Ch 1, sc in first unused lp on 2nd row below and in front lp of first sc at same time, *sc in next unused lp on 2nd row below and in front lp of next sc at same time, rep from * to last 2 sc, sc dec, turn. *(13 [14, 15] sc)*

## For Size 12 Months Only
**Row 71:** Sl st in first 3 sc, ch 1, *sc in next unused lp on 2nd row below and in front lp of next sc at same time, rep from * 9 times, turn. *(10 sc)*

**Row 72:** Ch 1, sc in first unused lp on 2nd row below and through both lps of first sc at same time, *sc in next unused lp on 2nd row below and through both lps of next sc at same time, rep from * across.

Fasten off and weave in ends.

Continue with Assembly.

## For Sizes 18 & 24 Months Only
**Row 77 [87]:** Rep row 3.

**Row 78 [88]:** Ch 1, sc in first unused lp on 2nd row below and in front lp of first sc at same time, *sc in next unused lp on 2nd row below and in front lp of next sc at same time, rep from * to last 2 sc, sc dec, turn. *(13 [14] sc)*

## For Size 18 Months Only
**Row 79:** Sl st in first 3 sc, ch 1, *sc in next unused lp on 2nd row below and in front lp of next sc at same time, rep from * 8 times, turn. *(10 sc)*

**Row 80:** Ch 1, sc in first unused lp on 2nd row below and through both lps of first sc at same time, *sc in next unused lp on 2nd row below and through both lps of next sc at same time, rep from * across.

Fasten off and weave in ends.

Continue with Assembly.

### For Size 24 Months Only

**Row 89:** Ch 1, sc in first unused lp on 2nd row below and in front lp of first sc at same time, *sc in next unused lp on 2nd row below and in front lp of next sc at same time, rep from * to last 2 sc, sc dec, turn. *(14 sc)*

**Row 90:** Rep row 3.

**Row 91:** Sl st in first 2 sc, ch 1, *sc in next unused lp on 2nd row below and in front lp of next sc at same time, rep from * 11 times, turn. *(12 sc)*

**Row 92:** Ch 1, sc in first unused lp on 2nd row below and through both lps of first sc at same time, *sc in next unused lp on 2nd row below and through both lps of next sc at same time, rep from * across.

Fasten off and weave in ends.

Continue with Assembly.

### Assembly

With tapestry needle and A, sew shoulder seams.

### Sleeves

**Rnd 1:** Holding piece with RS facing you, with size I hook and A, make slip knot on hook and join with sc in 1 underarm, work 30 [33, 39, 45] sc evenly sp around armhole, join in first sc, turn. *(31 [34, 40, 46] sc)*

**Rnd 2:** Ch 1, working in front lps only, sc in each sc, join in first sc, turn.

**Rnd 3:** Ch 1, sc in first unused lp on 2nd rnd below and in front lp of first sc at same time, *sc in next unused lp on 2nd rnd below and in front lp of next sc at same time, rep from * around, join in first sc, turn.

**Rnds 4–41 [4–47, 4–51, 4–54]:** Rep rnd 3.

**Rnd 42 [48, 52, 55]:** Ch 1, sc in first unused lp on 2nd rnd below and through both lps of first sc at same time, *sc in next unused lp on 2nd rnd below and through both lps of next sc at same time, rep from * across.

Fasten off and weave in ends.

Rep for 2nd Sleeve.

### Bottom Edging

**Row 1 (RS):** Holding piece with RS facing you and beg ch at top, with B make slip knot on size I hook and join with sc in unused lp of first ch, working in rem unused lps of beg ch, sc in each lp, turn. *(76 [80, 84, 88] sc)*

**Row 2:** Ch 1, sc in each sc, turn.

**Row 3:** Ch 1, sc in each sc.

### Right Front Band

**Row 1:** Ch 1, working in ends of rows across Right Rront, work 33 [35, 40, 44] sc evenly sp to row 59 [63, 69, 79], turn. *(33 [35, 40, 44] sc)*

**Row 2:** Ch 1, sc in each sc, turn.

**Rows 3–5:** Rep row 2. Fasten off.

### Left Front Band

**Row 1:** Holding piece with RS facing you, with B make slip knot on size I hook and join with sc in end of row 59 [63,

69, 79], working in ends of rows of Left Front, work 32 [34, 39, 43] sc evenly sp to row 3 of Bottom Edging, turn. *(33 [35, 40, 44] sc)*

**Row 2:** Ch 1, sc in each sc, turn.

### For Size 6 Months Only
**Row 3:** Ch 1, sc in first 2 sc, *ch 2—*button lp made*, sk next sc, sc in next 4 sc, rep from * 4 times, ch 2—*button lp made*, sk next sc, sc in last 3 sc, turn.

Continue with For All Sizes.

### For Size 12 Months Only
**Row 3:** Ch 1, sc in first 2 sc, *ch 2—*button lp made*, sk next sc, sc in next 5 sc, rep from * 4 times, ch 2—*button lp made*, sk next sc, sc in last 2 sc, turn.

Continue with For All Sizes.

### For Size 18 Months Only
**Row 3:** Ch 1, sc in first 2 sc, *ch 2—*button lp made*, sk next sc, sc in next 6 sc, rep from * 4 times, ch 2—*button lp made*, sk next sc, sc in last 2 sc, turn.

Continue with For All Sizes.

### For Size 24 Months Only
**Row 3:** Ch 1, sc in first 2 sc, *ch 2—*button lp made*, sk next sc, sc in next 5 sc, ch 2—*button lp made*, sk next sc, sc in next 6 sc, rep from * twice, sc in last 3 sc, turn.

Continue with For All Sizes.

### For All Sizes
**Row 4:** Ch 1, sc in each sc and in each ch-2 sp, turn.

**Row 5:** Ch 1, sc in each sc.

Fasten off and weave in ends.

## Collar
*Note: Collar is not worked across either front band.*

**Row 1:** Hold piece with RS facing you, with B make slip knot on size I hook and join with sc in first unused row of neck edge from Right Front Band, working across neck edge, work 40 [44, 48, 52 ] sc evenly spaced to Left Front Band, turn. *(40 [44, 48, 52] sc)*

**Row 2:** Ch 1, sc in each sc, turn.

**Row 3:** Ch 1, sc in first 3 sc, 2 sc in next sc, *sc in next 3 sc, 2 sc in next sc, rep from * across, turn. *(50 [55, 60, 65] sc)*

**Rows 4 & 5:** Rep row 2.

**Row 6:** Ch 1, sc in first 4 sc, 2 sc in next sc, *sc in next 4 sc, 2 sc in next sc, rep from * across, turn. *(60 [66, 72, 78] sc)*

### For Sizes 6 Months & 12 Months Only
**Row 7:** Ch 1, sc in each sc. Do not turn.

## Edging
Working around outer edge of Cardigan, sl st in end of each row and in each sc, join in first sl st.

Fasten off and weave in ends.

Continue with Sleeve Band.

### For Sizes 18 Months & 24 Months Only
**Row 7:** Ch 1, sc in each sc, turn.

**Row 8:** Rep row 7.

**Row 9:** Ch 1, sc in each sc. Do not turn.

## Edging

Working around outer edge of Cardigan, sl st in end of each row and in each sc, join in first sl st.

Fasten off and weave in ends.

Continue with Sleeve Band.

## Sleeve Band

**Rnd 1:** Holding piece with 1 Sleeve at top, with B make slip knot on size I hook and join with sc in first sc of last rnd of Sleeve, sc in each rem sc, join with sl st in first sc. *(31 [34, 40, 46] sc)*

**Rnd 2:** Ch 1, sc in each sc, join with sl st in first sc.

**Rnd 3:** Rep rnd 2.

**Rnd 4:** Sl st in each sc, join in joining sl st.

Fasten off and weave in ends.

Rep on rem Sleeve.

## Fish

**Row 1:** With size 7 hook and C, ch 10, sc in 2nd ch from hook and in each rem ch, turn. *(9 sc)*

**Row 2:** Ch 1, sc dec in first 2 sc, sc in each sc to last 2 sc, sc dec in last 2 sc, turn. *(7 sc)*

**Row 3:** Rep row 2. *(5 sc at end of row)*

**Row 4:** Ch 1, sc dec in first 2 sc, sc in next sc, sc dec, turn. *(3 sc)*

**Row 5:** Ch 1, draw up lp in each sc, yo and draw through all 4 lps on hook, turn.

**Row 6:** Ch 1, 3 sc in st, turn. *(3 sc)*

**Row 7:** Ch 1, 2 sc in first sc, sc in next sc, 2 sc in last sc, turn. *(5 sc)*

**Row 8:** Ch 1, 2 sc in first sc, sc in each sc to last sc, 2 sc in last sc, turn. *(7 sc)*

**Rows 9–12:** Rep row 8. *(15 sc at end of last row)*

**Row 13:** Ch 1, sc in each sc, turn.

**Rows 14–17:** Rep row 13.

**Row 18:** Ch 1, sc dec in first 2 sc, sc in each sc to last 2 sc, sc dec, turn. *(13 sc)*

**Rows 19–22:** Rep row 18. *(5 sc at end of last row)*

**Row 23:** Ch 1, sc dec in first 2 sc, sc in next sc, sc dec. Do not turn. *(3 sc)*

## Edging

Ch 1, working in ends of rows and in unused lps of beg ch, 2 sc in end of row 23, sc in each row to row 16, 2 sc in end of row 16, sc in end of row 15, 2 sc in end of row 14, sc in end of each row to row 1, 3 sc in end of row 1, sc in unused lp of each ch of beg ch, working across next side, 3 sc in end of row 1, sc in each row to row 14, 2 sc in end of row 14, sc in end of row 15, 2 sc in end of row 16, sc in each row to row 23, 2 sc in end of row 23, join in first sc of row 23.

Fasten off, leaving a 12-inch end for sewing.

## Finishing

With sewing needle and matching thread, sew buttons to Right Front Band.

Referring to photo for placement and with D, embroider eye and mouth on Fish. Sew Fish to Left Front of Cardigan. ∎

# BABY LETTER JACKET

*Easy stitches and simple construction make this letter-style jacket a quick and fun baby project.*

Design | Brandee Fondren

## Skill Level ◖■□▭ 
**EASY**

## Sizes
Instructions given fit size 6–12 months; changes for 18 months and 24 months are in [ ].

## Finished Measurements
**Chest:** 23 inches *(6–12 months)* [24 inches *(18 months)*, 25 inches *(24 months)*]]

## Materials
Worsted weight yarn (197 yds/85g per ball):
   1 [2, 2] ball(s) forest green
Bulky weight suede yarn (122 yds/85g per ball):
   1 [2, 2] ball(s) light brown
Sizes H/8/5mm and I/9/5.5mm crochet hooks or sizes needed to obtain gauge
Tapestry needle
Snaps (see Closure Options Guide on page 71)
Stitch marker

## Gauge
**Size H hook and worsted yarn:** 16 sc = 4 inches; 10 sc rows = 4 inches

**Size I hook and bulky yarn:** 13 sc = 4 inches; 14 sc rows = 4 inches

Take time to check gauge.

## Notes
Work in continuous rounds, do not turn or join unless otherwise stated.

Mark first stitch of each round.

This versatile little jacket is perfect for either boy or girl, depending on your colour choices. If desired, add a sew-on appliqué to highlight a favourite team or theme.

# Jacket

## Back
**Row 1:** With size H hook and forest green, ch 47 [49, 51], sc in 2nd ch from hook and in each ch across, turn. *(46 [48, 50] sc)*

**Rows 2–26 [2–27, 2–28]:** Ch 1, sc in each st across, turn.

**Row 27 [28, 29]:** Sl st in each of first 4 [5, 5] sts, ch 1, sc in each of next 37 [37, 39] sts, leaving rem sts unworked, turn. *(38 [38, 40] sc)*

**Rows 28–50 [29–51, 30–52]:** Ch 1, sc in each st across, turn. At end of last row, fasten off.

## First Front
**Row 1:** With size H hook and forest green, ch 26 [27, 28], sc in 2nd ch from hook and in each ch across, turn. *(25 [26, 27] sc)*

**Rows 2–26 [2–27, 2–28]:** Ch 1, sc in each st across, turn.

**Baby Letter Jacket**
Sample project was crocheted with Wool-Ease
(80 per cent acrylic, 20 per cent wool) and Suede
(100 per cent polyester) from Lion Brand.

**Row 27 [28, 29]:** Sk first st, sl st in each of first 3 [3, 4] sts, ch 1, sc in each st across, turn. *(21 [22, 22] sc)*

**Rows 28–41 [29–42, 30–43]:** Ch 1, sc in each st across, turn.

**Row 42 [43, 44]:** Ch 1, sc in each of next 16 [17, 17] sts, leaving rem sts unworked, turn. *(16 [17, 17] sc)*

**Row 43 [44, 45]:** Ch 1, **sc dec** *(see Stitch Guide on page 126)* in first 2 sts, sc in each st across, turn. *(15 [16, 16] sc)*

**Row 44 [45, 46]:** Ch 1, sc in each st across leaving last st unworked, turn. *(14 [15, 15] sc)*

**Rows 45 & 46 [46 & 47, 47 & 48]:** Rep rows 43 and 44 [44 and 45, 45 and 46]. *(12 [13, 13] sc at end of last row)*

**Row 47 [48, 49]:** Rep row 43 [44, 45]. *(11, [12, 12] sc)*

**Rows 48–50 [49–51, 50–52]:** Ch 1, sc in each st across, turn. At end of last row, fasten off.

## 2nd Front
Rep First Front reversing all shaping.

Sew shoulder and side seams.

## Trim
**Row 1:** Working across bottom edge in starting ch on opposite side of row 1 on Fronts and Back, join light brown with sc in first ch, sc in each ch across, turn. Fasten off.

**Row 2:** Join forest green with sc in first st, sc in each st across, turn.

**Row 3:** Ch 1, sc in each st across, turn. Fasten off.

**Row 4:** Join light brown with sc in first st, sc in each st across, turn. Fasten off.

## Sleeve
**Rnd 1:** With size I hook, join light brown with sc in last st before underarm, [sc dec in next 2 sts] 5 times, sc in end of every other row around shoulder, **do not join** *(see Notes on page 68)*.

**Rnd 2:** Sc dec in next 2 sts, sc in next st, sc dec in next 2 sts, sc in each st around.

**Rnds 3–25 [3–26, 3–27]:** Sc in each st around. At end of last rnd, fasten off.

**Rnd 26 [27, 28]:** Join forest green with sc in first st, [sc dec in next 2 sts, sc in next st] around.

**Rnd 27 [28, 29]:** Sc in each st around. Fasten off.

**Rnd 28 [29, 30]:** Join light brown with sc in any st, sc in each st around. Fasten off.

**Rnd 29 [30, 31]:** Join forest green with sc in any st, sc in each st around.

**Rnd 30 [31, 32]:** Sc in each st around. Fasten off.

Rep on rem armhole.

## Collar
**Row 1:** With size I hook, join light brown with sc in first st after unworked st at neck edge, evenly sp 39 sc around neck, ending in last st before 4 unworked sts, turn.

**Row 2:** Ch 1, sc in each st across, turn. Fasten off.

**Row 3:** Join forest green with sc in first st, sc in each st across, turn.

**Row 4:** Ch 1, sc in each st across, turn. Fasten off.

**Row 5:** Join light brown with sc in first st, sc in each st across.

**Row 6:** Ch 1, sc in each st across. Fasten off.

# Closure Options Guide

### Shiny Backed Snaps

This closure looks perfect with this project. It is inexpensive and easy to install. For this closure option, follow the manufacturer's directions to place 4 snaps evenly spaced along the front of the Jacket. Try to avoid "heavy-duty snaps" as they are sometimes difficult to open, and use care when opening this type of snap as it tends to be rough on the fabric and may pull out. This is a great option when the closure will be more for style than function.

### Magnetic Snaps

This closure is easier on the fabric but adds weight to the front of the Jacket and is more expensive than traditional snaps. You may choose to install false shiny backed snaps along the front of the Jacket before stitching it closed to give it that authentic look. With this option, you will need to cover the snap backs by making 2 Snap Cover Flaps following the pattern below. Evenly place 4 female sides along the front left facing up and stitch the cover flap closed, hiding the snap backs. Install the male sides on the Cover Flap facing down, and then stitch it closed.

### Snap Cover Flap

Crochet the Cover Flap, and then, without breaking the yarn, attach it to the Front of the Jacket using these instructions. Once you have crocheted 2 rows, measure it against your Jacket Front to make sure it fits and covers your snap backs with plenty of room to stitch it closed.

**Row 1:** With size H hook and forest green, ch 39 [41, 43], sc in 2nd st from hook and in each ch across, turn. *(38 [40, 42] sc)*

**Rows 2–6:** Ch 1, sc in each st across.

**Attaching row:** Ch 1, with WS facing, sc through Flap and Front of Jacket in each st along the length of the Front. Leaving 20-inch end for attaching the rest of the Flap, fasten off. Pull end through lp of last st.

Once the snaps are installed, st the perimeter of the Flap to the Jacket Front, taking care to use the **back lps** *(see Stitch Guide on page 126)* so your sts are not seen from the front of the Jacket. With the rem of end, add additional sts in a zigzag pattern to give extra support to your snaps. Weave in the end. ■

# LITTLE MOUNTAIN MAN

*Baby will be snug and cozy wrapped in this cute layette.*

Design | Natalie Garrison

## Skill Level

**EASY**

## Sizes

Instructions given fit smallest size; changes for larger sizes are in [ ].

Jacket: 0–3 months *(small)* [3–6 months *(medium)*, 6–9 months *(large)*]

Hat: 14¼ [15, 16½] inches in circumference

Mittens: 3 [3¼, 3½] inches long

Bunting: 14 [14½, 16] inches across

## Finished Measurements

**Chest:** 17¾ inches *(small)*, [18½ inches *(medium)*, 20½ inches *(large)*]

## Materials

Worsted weight yarn (364 yds/198g per skein):
   2 skeins light blue

Worsted weight yarn (4 oz/210 yds/113g per ball):
   1 ball white

Size F/5/3.75mm [G/6/4mm, H/8/5mm] crochet hook or size needed to obtain gauge

Tapestry needle

Sewing needle

10 nailhead decorative ⁷⁄₁₆-inch snaps

Blue sewing thread

## Gauge

**Size F hook:** 7 hdc = 2 inches; 5 hdc rows = 2 inches [**Size G hook:** 10 hdc = 3 inches; 6 hdc rows = 2 inches; **Size H hook:** 6 hdc = 2 inches; 4 hdc rows = 2 inches]

Take time to check gauge.

## Notes

Chain-2 at beginning of half double crochet row does not count as a half double crochet unless otherwise stated.

Use F hook for small size, G hook for medium size, and H hook for large size.

# Jacket

## Back

**Row 1 (RS):** With light blue, ch 33, hdc in 2nd ch from hook and in each ch across, turn. *(32 hdc)*

**Rows 2–20:** Ch 2 *(see Notes)*, hdc in each st across, turn.

### First Shoulder

**Row 1:** Ch 2, hdc in each of first 8 sts, **hdc dec** *(see Stitch Guide on page 126)* in next 2 sts, hdc in next st, leaving rem sts unworked, turn. *(10 hdc)*

**Row 2:** Ch 2, hdc in first st and in each st across. Fasten off.

### Little Mountain Man
Sample projects were crocheted with Red Heart Super Saver (100 per cent acrylic) from Coats & Clark and Baby Bee Lambie Pie (100 per cent polyamide) from Hobby Lobby.

## 2nd Shoulder

**Row 1:** Sk next 10 sts on last row of Back, join with sl st in next st, ch 2, hdc in same st, hdc dec in next 2 sts, hdc in each of last 8 sts, turn. *(10 hdc)*

**Row 2:** Ch 2, hdc in first st and in each st across. Fasten off.

## Trim

Working in starting back strands of hdc on row 14, join white with sl st in first st, ch 2, hdc in same st as sl st and in each st across. Fasten off.

## Left Front

**Row 1 (RS):** With light blue, ch 16, hdc 2nd ch from hook and in each ch across, turn. *(15 hdc)*

**Rows 2–20:** Ch 2, hdc in first st and in each st across, turn.

**Row 21:** Ch 2, hdc in each of first 8 sts, hdc dec in next 2 sts, hdc in next st, leaving rem sts unworked, turn. *(10 hdc)*

**Row 22:** Ch 2, hdc in first st and in each st across. Fasten off.

**Row 23:** Working in back strands of hdc on row 14, join white with sl st in first st, ch 2, hdc in same st as last sl st and in each st across. Fasten off.

## Right Front

**Rows 1–20:** Rep rows 1–20 of Left Front.

**Row 21:** Sl st in each of first 5 sts, ch 2, hdc in same st as last sl st and in each of next 7 sts, hdc dec in next 2 sts, hdc in last st, turn. *(10 hdc)*

**Row 22:** Ch 2, hdc in first st and in each st across. Fasten off.

**Row 23:** Working in back strands of hdc on row 14, join white with sl st in first st, ch 2, hdc in same st as first sl st and in each st across. Fasten off.

## Left Placket

**Row 1:** With RS facing, join light blue with sc in end of row 21 on Left Front, evenly sp 26 sc across ends of rows to bottom corner, turn. *(27 sc)*

**Rows 2 & 3:** Ch 1, sc in each st across, turn. Fasten off at end of last row.

## Right Placket

**Row 1:** With RS facing, join light blue with sc in end of row 1 on Right Front, evenly sp 26 sc across to top corner, turn. *(27 sc)*

**Rows 2 & 3:** Ch 1, sc in each st across, turn. Fasten off at end of last row.

Sew shoulder seams.

## Sleeve

**Make 2**

**Row 1:** With light blue, ch 24, hdc in 2nd ch from hook and in each ch across, turn. *(23 hdc)*

**Rows 2 & 3:** Ch 2, hdc in each st across, turn.

**Row 4:** Ch 2, hdc in first st, 2 hdc in next st, hdc in each st across to last 2 sts, 2 hdc in next st, hdc in last st, turn. *(25 hdc)*

**Rows 5–7:** Ch 2, hdc in first st and in each st across, turn.

**Row 8:** Rep row 4. *(27 hdc)*

**Rows 9–11:** Ch 2, hdc in first st and in each st across, turn.

**Row 12:** Rep row 4. *(29 hdc)*

**Row 13:** Ch 1, sc in each st across. Fasten off.

Matching centre of last row on Sleeves to shoulder seams, sew Sleeves in place. Sew Sleeve and side seams.

## Sleeve Trim

**Rnd 1:** Working around 1 Sleeve opening, join white with sc in seam, sc in each st around, join with sl st in beg sc. *(24 sc)*

**Rnd 2:** Ch 1, sc in each st around, join with sl st in beg sc. Fasten off.

Rep on other Sleeve opening.

## Body Trim

**Rnd 1:** Working around entire outer edge, join light blue with sc at centre Back, evenly sp sc around, join with sl st in beg sc. Fasten off.

**Rnd 2:** Join white with sc in first st, sc in each st around, join with sl st in beg sc.

**Rnd 3:** Ch 1, sc in each st around, join in beg sc. Fasten off.

## Collar

**Row 1:** Sk first 3 sts on neck edge, join white with sc in next st, sc in each st across neck edge, leaving last 3 sts at opposite end unworked, turn.

**Rows 2–6:** Ch 1, 2 sc in first st, sc in each st across with 2 sc in last st, turn. Fasten off at end of last row.

Placing top snap 2 inches below bottom edge of Collar, attach 3 snaps evenly sp down front opening with decorative half on left front.

# Mitten

**Make 2**

## Body

**Rnd 1:** With light blue, ch 5, sc in 2nd ch from hook, sc in each of next 2 chs, 3 sc in last ch, working on opposite side of ch, sc in each of next 2 chs, 2 sc in last ch, **do not join**. *(10 sc)*

**Rnd 2:** 2 sc in next st, sc in each of next 2 sts, 2 sc in each of next 3 sts, sc in each of next 2 sts, 2 sc in each of last 2 sts. *(16 sc)*

**Rnd 3:** Sc in each st around.

**Rnd 4:** [Sc in each of next 7 sts, 2 sc in next st] twice. *(18 sc)*

**Rnds 5–12:** Sc in each st around.

**Rnd 13:** [Sc in each of next 7 sts, **sc dec** *(see Stitch Guide on page 126)* in next 2 sts] around. *(16 dc)*

**Rnd 14:** [Sc in next st, 2 sc in next st] around. *(24 sc)*

**Rnd 15:** Sc in each st around, join with sl st in beg sc. Fasten off.

**Rnd 16:** Join white with sc in first st, sc in each st around, join with sl st in beg sc. Fasten off.

## Mitten Keeper

Join light blue with sc in row 15 of 1 Mitten, ch 51, sl st in corresponding st on opposite Mitten, sl st in 2nd ch from hook and in each ch across. Sl st in same st as first sl st. Fasten off.

# Hat

## Body

**Rnd 1:** With light blue, ch 3, 10 hdc in 3rd ch from hook, join with sl st in 2nd ch of beg ch-2, turn. *(10 hdc)*

**Rnd 2:** Ch 2, 2 hdc in each hdc around, join with sl st in 2nd ch of beg ch-2, turn. *(20 hdc)*

**Rnd 3:** Ch 2, [2 hdc in next hdc, hdc in next hdc] around, join with sl st in 2nd ch of beg ch-2, turn. *(30 hdc)*

**Rnd 4:** Ch 2, [2 hdc in next hdc, hdc in each of next 2 hdc] around, join with sl st in 2nd ch of beg ch-2, turn. *(40 hdc)*

**Rnd 5:** Ch 2, hdc in each hdc around, join with sl st in 2nd ch of beg ch-2, turn.

**Rnd 6:** Ch 2, [2 hdc in next hdc, hdc in each of next 3 hdc] around, join in 2nd ch of beg ch-3, turn. *(50 hdc)*

**Rnds 7–12:** Ch 2, hdc in each hdc around, join with sl st in 2nd ch of beg ch-2, turn. Fasten off at end of last rnd.

## Back Flap

**Row 1:** Join light blue with sl st in first of 6 sts before joining, ch 2, hdc in same st as ch-2, hdc in each of next 5 sts, hdc in next joining, hdc in each of next 6 sts, turn. *(13 hdc)*

**Row 2:** Ch 2, hdc in first st and in each st across, turn.

**Row 3:** Ch 2, hdc in first st, hdc dec *(see Stitch Guide on page 126)* in next 2 sts, hdc in each st across to last 3 sts, hdc dec in next 2 sts, hdc in last st. Fasten off.

## First Ear Flap

**Row 1:** Sk next st on last row of Body, join light blue with sl st in next st, ch 2, hdc in same st, hdc dec in next 2 sts, hdc in each of next 6 sts, hdc dec in next 2 sts, hdc in last st, leaving rem sts unworked, turn. *(10 hdc)*

**Row 2:** Ch 2, hdc in first st, hdc dec in next 2 sts, hdc in each of next 4 sts, hdc dec in next 2 sts, hdc in last st, turn. *(8 hdc)*

**Row 3:** Ch 2, hdc in first st, hdc dec in next 2 sts, hdc in each of next 2 sts, hdc dec in next 2 sts, hdc in last st, turn. *(6 hdc)*

**Row 4:** Ch 2, hdc in first st, [hdc dec in each of next 2 sts] twice, hdc in last st, turn. *(4 hdc)*

**Row 5:** Ch 2, hdc in first st, hdc dec in next 2 sts, hdc in last st, turn. *(3 hdc)*

**Row 6:** Ch 2, pull up a lp in each of first 3 sts, yo, pull through 4 lps on hook. Fasten off.

## 2nd Ear Flap

**Row 1:** Sk next 12 sts on last row of Body, join light blue with sl st in next st, ch 2, hdc in same st, hdc dec in next 2 sts, hdc in each of next 6 sts, hdc dec in next 2 sts, hdc in next st, leaving rem sts unworked, turn. *(10 hdc)*

**Rows 2–6:** Rep rows 2–6 of First Ear Flap.

## Front Flap

**Row 1:** Working in 12 sk sts between Ear Flaps, join white with sc in first st, sc in each of next 11 sts, turn. *(12 sc)*

**Rows 2–6:** Ch 1, sc in each st across, turn.

**Rows 7 & 8:** Ch 1, **sc dec** *(see Stitch Guide on page 126)* in first 2 sts, sc in each st across to last 2 sts, sc dec in last 2 sts, turn. Fasten off at end of last row. *(8 sc at end of last row)*

**Row 9:** Join light blue with sc in end of first row, sc in end of each row and each st around to opposite end of row 1. Fasten off.

Fold Front Flap up and tack to Body.

## Trim

Join white with sc in st on 1 side of Front Flap, sc in each st and in end of each row around to opposite side of Front Flap. Fasten off.

## Ties

Join light blue with sl st in centre of st on row 6 of 1 Ear Flap, ch 51, sc in 2nd ch from hook and in each ch across, sl st in same st on Ear Flap. Fasten off.

Rep on other Ear Flap.

Attach decorative half of 1 snap to each Ear Flap above Ties.

# Bunting

## Base

**Rnd 1:** With light blue, ch 26, 5 hdc in 2nd ch from hook, hdc in each of next 23 chs, 5 hdc in last ch, working on opposite side of ch, hdc in each of next 23 chs, join with sl st in first hdc, **turn.** *(56 hdc)*

**Rnd 2:** Ch 2, 2 hdc in first st, hdc in each of next 23 sts, 2 hdc in each of next 5 sts, hdc in each of next 23 sts, 2 hdc in each of last 4 sts, join with sl st in 2nd ch of beg ch-2. *(66 hdc)*

**Rnd 3:** Ch 2, [2 hdc in next st, hdc in next st] 4 times, hdc in each of next 23 sts, [2 hdc in next st, hdc in next st] 5 times, hdc in each of next 23 sts, 2 hdc in next st hdc last st, join in 2nd ch of beg ch 2, turn. *(76 hdc)*

**Rnd 4:** Ch 2, 2 hdc in next st, hdc in each of next 25 sts, [2 hdc in next st, hdc in each of next 2 sts] 5 times, hdc in each of next 23 sts, [2 hdc in next st, hdc in each of next 2 sts] 4 times, join in 2nd ch of beg ch-2, turn. *(86 hdc)*

**Rnd 5:** Ch 2, [2 hdc in next st, hdc in each of next 3 sts] 4 times, hdc in each of next 23 sts, [2 hdc in next st, hdc in each of next 3 sts] 5 times, hdc in each of next 23 sts, 2 hdc in next st, hdc in each of last 3 sts, join in beg ch-2, **do not turn.** *(96 hdc)*

**Rnd 6:** Ch 1, sc in each hdc around, join with sl st in beg sc.

**Rnd 7:** Working this rnd in **back lps** *(see Stitch Guide on page 126)* sc in each st around, join with sl st in beg sc, turn. Fasten off.

**Row 8:** Now working in rows, join light blue in first st of last 9 sts, ch 2, hdc in same st as ch-2, hdc in each st across, turn. *(96 hdc)*

**Rows 9–36:** Ch 2, hdc in first st and in each st across, turn. Fasten off at end of last row.

**Row 37:** For **Flap**, sk first 18 sts, join light blue with sl st in next st, ch 2, hdc in same st as ch 2, **hdc dec** *(see Stitch Guide on page 126)* in next 3 sts, hdc in each of next 52 sts, hdc dec in next 3 sts, hdc in next st, leaving the last 18 sts unworked, turn. *(56 hdc)*

**Rows 38–40:** Ch 2, hdc in first st, [hdc dec in next 2 sts] twice, hdc in each st across to last 5 sts, [hdc dec in next 2 sts] twice, hdc in last st, turn. *(44 hdc at end of last row)*

**Rows 41–79:** Ch 2, hdc in first st and in each st across, turn.

**Rows 80–85:** Ch 2, hdc in first st, hdc dec in next 2 sts, hdc in each st across to last 3 sts, hdc dec in next 2 sts, hdc in last st, turn. *(32 hdc at end of last row)*

**Rows 86–90:** Rep row 38. *(12 hdc at end of last row)*

**Row 91:** Ch 2, hdc in each st across, turn. Fasten off.

## Right Placket

**Row 1:** Working on RS, join light blue with sc in end of row 1, evenly sp 39 sc across to row 29, turn. *(40 sc)*

**Row 2:** Working this row in **front lps** *(see Stitch Guide on page 126)*, ch 1, sc in each st across, turn.

**Row 3:** Ch 1, sc in each st across. Fasten off.

## Left Placket

**Row 1:** Working on left side, join light blue with sc in end of row 29, evenly sp 39 sc across to row 1, turn. *(40 sc)*

**Row 2:** Working this row in front lps, ch 1, sc in each st across, turn.

**Row 3:** Ch 1, sc in each st across, turn.

**Row 4:** Working across entire outer edge, ch 1, evenly sp sc across Plackets and around top of Bunting to last st of Right Placket. Fasten off.

## Base Trim

**Rnd 1:** Working in rem lps of rnd 6 on Base, join white with sc in any st, sc in each st around, join with sl st in beg sc, **do not turn.**

**Rnd 2:** Ch 1, sc in each st around, join with sl st in beg sc. Fasten off.

## Body Trim

**Row 1:** Working in rem lps of row 1 on Plackets and around top of Bunting *(see photo on page 73)*, join white with sl st in first st on Right Placket, sc in each st around, turn.

**Row 2:** Ch 1, sc in each st around. Fasten off.

Placing lowest snap 1½-inch from bottom of Plackets, attach 5 snaps evenly spaced down Plackets with decorative half on Left Placket.

Overlap Left Placket over Right Placket and tack tog at bottom edge. ∎

# SWEET POSIES

*Easy to stitch, this beautiful afghan
will be a treasured baby keepsake.*

Design | Joyce Nordstrom

## Skill Level

**EASY**

## Finished Size
Approximately 37½ x 38½ inches

## Materials
DK weight yarn (solids: 575 yds/198g; prints:
    430 yds/170g per skein): 4 skeins
    variegated (A), 1 skein lime (B)
Size G/6/4mm crochet hook or size needed to
    obtain gauge
Tapestry needle

## Gauge
16 hdc = 4 inches
Take time to check gauge.

## Special Stitches
**Front post double crochet (fpdc):** Yo, insert hook from
front to back to front around **post** *(see Stitch Guide on
page 126)* of st indicated, draw lp through, [yo, draw
through 2 lps on hook] twice. Always sk st on working row
behind fpdc.

**V-stitch (V-st):** In sp indicated work (hdc, ch 1, hdc).

## Bottom Border
**Row 1 (RS):** With A, ch 163, hdc in 2nd ch from hook and
in each rem ch, turn. *(162 hdc)*

**Row 2:** Ch 2, hdc in each hdc, turn.

Rep row 2 until piece measures 5 inches from beg.

## Centre
**Foundation row:** Ch 2, hdc in first 19 hdc, ***fpdc** (see
Special Stitches)* around next st 1 row below, hdc in next
hdc, rep from * to last 20 hdc, fpdc around next st 1 row
below, hdc in last 19 hdc, turn.

**Row 1 (WS):** Ch 2, hdc in first 20 sts, [sk next 2 sts, **V-st**
*(see Special Stitches)* in next st] 40 times; sk next 2 sts, hdc
in next 20 sts, turn.

**Row 2 (RS):** Ch 2, hdc in first 19 hdc, fpdc around next fpdc
2 rows below, [V-st between next 2 V-sts] 39 times, fpdc
around next fpdc 2 rows below, hdc in last 19 hdc, turn.

**Row 3:** Ch 2, hdc first 20 sts, V-st in sp between last st
worked and next V-st, [V-st between next 2 V-sts]
38 times, sk last V-st, V-st in sp between sk V-st and
next st, hdc in next 20 sts, turn.

Rep rows 2 and 3 until piece measures approximately
32 inches from beg, ending with a RS row.

**Last row:** Ch 2, hdc in first 20 sts, sc in each hdc and in
each ch–1 sp to last 20 sts, hdc in last 20 sts, turn.

## Top Border
**Row 1 (RS):** Ch 2, hdc in first 19 hdc, *fpdc around next st
1 row below, hdc in next sc, rep from * to last 20 hdc, fpdc
around next st 1 row below, hdc in last 19 hdc, turn.

**Row 2:** Ch 2, hdc in each st, turn.

**Row 3:** Ch 2, hdc in each hdc, turn.

Rep row 3 until Top Border measures same as Bottom Border, ending with a WS row. At end of last row, ch 1, turn.

## Edging
Working around piece, sc evenly across each side to first sc, join in first sc.

Fasten off and weave in ends.

## Inside Trim
Holding afghan with RS facing you and 1 short end at top, join B around last fpdc in upper left-hand corner, ch 1, working left to right, *work **reverse sc** *(see Stitch Guide on page 126)* around next fpdc, ch 2, rep from * around, join in first reverse sc.

## Outside Edging
**Row 1 (RS):** Holding afghan with RS facing you and 1 short end at top, join B in last st in upper left-hand corner, ch 1, working left to right, work reverse sc in same st, *ch 2, sk next st, reverse sc in next st, rep from * around, join with sl st in first reverse sc.

**Row 2:** Ch 4, *sc in next ch-2 sp, ch 4, rep from * around, join with sl st in joining sl st.

**Row 3:** Ch 5, *sc in next ch-4 sp, ch 5, rep from * around, join with sl st in joining sl st.

Fasten off and weave in ends.

## Small Flower
### Make 19

With B, ch 5, join to form ring, ch 3, dc in ring, ch 3, [sl st in next ch, ch 3, dc in ring, ch 3] 4 times, join with sl st in joining sl st.

Fasten off and weave in ends.

## Large Flower
### Make 11

With B, ch 6, join to form ring, ch 3, dc in ring, ch 3, [sl st in next ch, ch 3, dc in ring, ch 3] 5 times, join with sl st in joining sl st.

Fasten off and weave in ends.

## Finishing
Referring to photo for placement and with tapestry needle and B, sew Flowers to afghan as desired. ∎

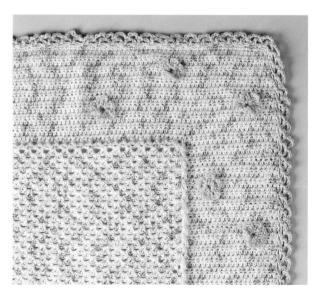

### Sweet Posies
Sample project was crocheted with Red Heart Soft Baby (100 per cent acrylic) from Coats & Clark.

# SOFT AS A CLOUD

*With its exquisite pattern, this blanket will be treasured for years to come.*

Design | Della Brenneise

## Skill Level

## Finished Size
33½ x 37½ inches

## Materials
DK weight yarn (165 yds/70g per skein):
   4 skeins blue, 3 skeins white
Size G/6/4mm crochet hook or size needed
   to obtain gauge

## Gauge
7 sc = 2 inches; 8 sc rows = 2 inches
Take time to check gauge.

## Special Stitch
**Long double crochet (long dc):** Dc in corresponding st 3 rows below, sk next st on last row behind long dc.

## Blanket
**Row 1:** With blue, ch 120, sc in 2nd ch from hook and in each ch across, turn. *(119 sc)*

**Rows 2–10:** Ch 1, sc in each st across, turn. Fasten off at end of last row.

**Row 11:** Join white with sc in first st, [long dc *(see Special Stitch),* sc in next st] across, turn. *(60 sc, 59 dc)*

**Row 12:** Ch 1, sc in each st across. Fasten off. *(119 sc)*

**Row 13:** Join blue with sc in first st, sc in each st across, turn. *(119 sc)*

**Rows 14–22:** Ch 1, sc in each st across, turn. Fasten off at end of last row.

**Row 23:** Join white with sc in first st, [long dc, sc in next st] across, turn. *(60 sc, 59 dc)*

**Row 24:** Ch 1, sc in each st across. Fasten off. *(119 sc)*

**Rows 25–108:** [Rep rows 13 to 24 consecutively] 7 times.

**Rows 109–118:** Rep rows 13 to 22.

## Border
**Rnd 1:** Now working in rnds around entire outer edge in sts and in ends of rows, join white with sc in any st, evenly sp sc around, with 3 sc in each corner st, join with sl st in beg sc.

**Rnds 2–6:** Ch 1, sc in each st around with 3 sc in each centre corner st, join with sl st in beg sc. Fasten off at end of last rnd.

**Rnd 7:** Join blue with sc in any st, long dc, *[sc in next st, long dc] across to 3 sts before next centre corner st, sc in next st, long dc, [sc in next st, long dc in same st as last long dc] twice, rep from * 3 times, [sc in next st, long dc] around, join with sl st in beg sc. Fasten off. ■

## Soft as a Cloud

Sample project was crocheted
with Red Heart Sport (100 per
cent acrylic) from Coats & Clark.

# ELEGANCE

*Celebrate a new arrival with
this perfect keepsake gift.*

Design | Lucille LaFlamme

## Skill Level

**INTERMEDIATE**

## Finished Size
37 x 39 inches

## Materials
DK weight yarn (575 yds/198g per skein):
  2 skeins lilac
Size G/6/4mm crochet hook or size needed
  to obtain gauge

## Gauge
9 dc = 2½ inches; 2 dc rows = 1 inch
Take time to check gauge.

## Notes
Chains are not counted as stitches.

Chain-3 at beginning of row or round counts as first double crochet unless otherwise stated.

Join with slip stitch as indicated unless otherwise stated.

## Special Stitch
**Shell:** 5 dc in place indicated.

## Blanket

**Row 1:** Ch 127, dc in 4th ch from hook *(first 3 chs count as first dc)* and in each ch across, turn. *(125 dc)*

**Row 2:** Ch 3 *(see Notes)*, dc in each st across, turn.

**Row 3:** Ch 3, dc in each of next 4 sts, *sk next 2 sts, **shell** *(see Special Stitch)* in next st, sk next 2 sts, dc in next st, ch 1, sk next st, dc in next st, sk next 2 sts, shell in next st, sk next 2 sts**, dc in each of next 8 sts, ch 1, sk next 2 sts, 3 dc in next st, ch 1, sk next 2 sts, dc in each of next 8 sts, rep from * across, ending last rep at **, dc in each of last 5 sts, turn. *(8 shells, 10 ch-1 sps, 75 dc)*

**Row 4:** Ch 3, dc in each of next 4 sts, *shell in centre dc of next shell, sk last 2 sts of same shell, dc in next st, ch 1, sk next ch-1 sp, dc in next st, shell in centre dc of next shell, sk last 2 sts of same shell, dc in each of next 5 sts**, ch 3, sk next 3 sts, 2 dc in next ch-1 sp, 2 dc in next st, 3 dc in next st, 2 dc in next st, 2 dc in next ch-1 sp, ch 3, sk next 3 sts, dc in each of next 5 sts, rep from * across, ending last rep at **, turn.

**Row 5:** Ch 3, dc in each of next 4 sts, *shell in centre dc of next shell, sk last 2 sts of same shell, dc in next st, ch 1, dc in next st, shell in centre dc of next shell, sk last 2 sts of same shell**, dc in each of next 4 sts, ch 3, sk next st, dc in next st, [ch 1, dc in next st] 10 times, ch 3, sk next st, dc in each of next 4 sts, rep from * across, ending last rep at **, dc in each of last 5 sts, turn.

Elegance
Sample project was crocheted with
Red Heart Soft Baby (100 per cent
acrylic) from Coats & Clark.

**Row 6:** Ch 3, dc in each of next 4 sts, *shell in centre dc of next shell, sk last 2 sts of same shell, dc in next st, ch 1, dc in next st, shell in centre dc of next shell, sk last 2 sts of same shell**, dc in each of next 3 sts, ch 3, sk next st and next ch sp, [sc in next ch-1 sp, ch 3] 10 times, sk next ch sp and next st, dc in each of next 3 sts, rep from * across, ending last rep at **, dc in each of last 5 sts, turn.

**Rows 7–9:** Ch 3, dc in each of next 4 sts, *shell in centre dc of next shell, sk last 2 sts of same shell, dc in next st, ch 1, dc in next st, shell in centre dc of next shell, sk last 2 sts of same shell**, dc in each of next 3 sts, ch 3, sk next ch sp, sc in next ch sp, [ch 3, sc in next ch sp] across to ch sp before next dc group, ch 3, sk next ch sp, dc in each of next 3 sts, rep from * across, ending last rep at **, dc in each of last 5 sts, turn.

**Rows 10 & 11:** Ch 3, dc in each of next 4 sts, *shell in centre dc of next shell, sk last 2 sts of same shell, dc in next st, ch 1, dc in next st, shell in centre dc of next shell, sk last 2 sts of same shell**, dc in each of next 3 sts, ch 4, sk next ch sp, sc in next ch sp, [ch 3, sc in next ch sp] across to ch sp before next dc group, ch 4, sk next ch sp, dc in each of next 3 sts, rep from * across, ending last rep at **, dc in each of last 5 sts, turn.

**Row 12:** Ch 3, dc in each of next 4 sts, *shell in centre dc of next shell, sk last 2 sts of same shell, dc in next st, ch 1, dc in next st, shell in centre dc of next shell, sk last 2 sts of same shell**, dc in each of next 3 sts, ch 5, sk next ch-4 sp, sc in next ch sp, [ch 3, sc in next ch sp] 3 times, ch 5, sk next ch sp, dc in each of next 3 sts, rep from * across, ending last rep at **, dc in each of last 5 sts, turn.

**Row 13:** Ch 3, dc in each of next 4 sts, *shell in centre dc of next shell, sk last 2 sts of same shell, dc in next st, ch 1, dc in next st, shell in centre dc of next shell, sk last 2 sts of same shell**, dc in each of next 3 sts, dc in each of next 2 chs, ch 4, sc in next ch sp, [ch 3, sc in next ch sp] twice, ch 4, sk next 3 chs, dc in each of next 2 chs, dc in each of next 3 sts, rep from * across, ending last rep at **, dc in each of last 5 sts, turn.

**Row 14:** Ch 3, dc in each of next 4 sts, *shell in centre dc of next shell, sk last 2 sts of same shell, dc in next st, ch 1, dc in next st, shell in centre dc of next shell, sk last 2 sts of same shell, dc in each of next 5 sts**, dc in each of next 2 chs, ch 4, sc in next ch sp, ch 3, sc in next ch sp, ch 4, sk next 2 chs, dc in each of next 2 chs, dc in each of next 5 sts, rep from * across, ending last rep at **, turn.

**Row 15:** Ch 3, dc in each of next 4 sts, *shell in centre dc of next shell, sk last 2 sts of same shell, dc in next st, ch 1, dc in next st, shell in centre dc of next shell, sk last 2 sts of same shell**, dc in each of next 7 sts, dc in each of next 2 chs, ch 1, dc in next ch sp, ch 1, sk next 2 chs, dc in each of next 2 chs, dc in each of next 7 sts, rep from * across, ending last rep at **, dc in each of last 5 sts, turn.

**Row 16:** Ch 3, dc in each of next 4 sts, *shell in centre dc of next shell, sk last 2 sts of same shell, dc in next st, ch 1, dc in next st, shell in centre dc of next shell, sk last 2 sts of same shell**, dc in each of next 21 sts and ch sps, rep from * across, ending last rep at **, dc in each of last 5 sts, turn.

**Row 17:** Ch 3, dc in each of next 4 sts, *shell in centre dc of next shell, sk last 2 sts of same shell, dc in next st, ch 1, dc in next st, shell in centre dc of next shell, sk last 2 sts of same shell**, dc in each of next 8 sts, ch 1, sk next 2 sts, 3 dc in next st, ch 1, sk next 2 sts, dc in each of next 8 sts, rep from * across, ending last rep at **, dc in each of last 5 sts, turn.

**Rows 18–71:** [Rep rows 4–17 consecutively] 4 times, ending last rep with row 15.

**Row 72:** Ch 3, dc in each dc, in each dc of each shell and in each ch sp across, turn.

**Row 73:** Ch 3, dc in each st across, **do not turn.**

## Border

**Rnd 1:** Now working in rnds, in ends of rows and in sts, ch 1, sc in end of first row, [ch 3, sc in end of next row] across, ch 3 *(corner)*, working in starting ch on opposite side of row 1, sc in first ch, [ch 3, sk next ch, sc in next ch] across, ch 3 *(corner)*, sc in end of first row, [ch 3, sc in end of next row] across, ch 3 *(corner)*, sc in first st, [ch 3, sk next st, sc in next st] across, ch 3 *(corner)*, **join** *(see Notes on page 84)* in beg sc.

**Rnd 2:** Sl st in next ch, ch 1, sc in next ch, [ch 3, sc in next ch sp] around, join in beg sc.

**Rnd 3:** Sl st in next ch, ch 1, sc in next ch, [ch 3, sc in next ch sp] around with (sc, ch 3, sc) in each corner ch sp, join in beg sc.

**Rnd 4:** Ch 1, sc in first st, *[5 dc in next st, sc in next st] across long edge, [3 dc in next st**, sc in next st] across short edge, rep from * around, ending last rep at **, join in beg sc. Fasten off. ∎

# GRANDMA'S DOUBLE DELIGHT

*Stitch this delightful afghan,*
*one block at a time.*

Design | Elaine Bartlett

## Skill Level

■■□□ **EASY**

## Finished Size

Approximately 30 x 36 inches

## Materials

Worsted weight yarn (364 yds/198g per skein):
   2 balls white (A), 1 skein each light blue (B),
   baby pink (C), pale yellow (D) and pale green (E)
Size I/9/5.5mm crochet hook or size needed
   to obtain gauge
Tapestry needle

## Gauge

Motif = 4½ x 4½ inches
Take time to check gauge.

## Special Stitch

**Long double crochet (long dc):** Dc in corresponding st 3
rows below, sk next st on last row behind long dc.

## Motif

**Make 7 each of motifs A–F**

**Rnd 1 (RS):** With A, ch 4, join with sl st to form ring, ch 3
*(counts as a dc)*, 2 dc in ring, ch 2, in ring work [3 dc, ch 2]
3 times, join with sl st in first sc. Fasten off. *(12 dc)*

**Rnd 2:** With 2nd colour, make slip knot on hook and join
with sc in **back lp** *(see Stitch Guide on page 126)* only of

first dc of any 3-dc group, sc in back lp of next 2 dc, *3 sc
in next ch-2 sp—*corner made*, sc in back lp of next 3 dc, rep
from * twice, 3 sc in next ch-2 sp—*corner made,* join with sl
st in first sc. Fasten off. *(24 sc)*

**Rnd 3:** With 3rd colour, make slip knot on hook and join
with sc in back lp of 3rd sc of any corner, *[dc in unused
**front lp** *(see Stitch Guide on page 126)* of next dc on rnd 1,
sk next sc on working rnd behind dc just made, sc in back
lp of next sc] twice, corner in next sc, sc in back lp of next
sc, rep from * twice, [dc in unused front lp of next dc on
rnd 1, sk next sc on working rnd behind dc just made, sc in
back lp of next sc] twice, corner in next sc, join with sl st in
first sc. Fasten off. *(32 sts)*

**Rnd 4:** With 4th colour, make slip knot on hook and join
with sc in back lp of 3rd sc of any corner, *[dc in unused
front lp of next st 1 rnd below, sk next st on working rnd
behind dc just made, sc in back lp of next st] 3 times,
corner in next sc, sc in back lp of next st, rep from * twice,
[dc in unused front lp of next st 1 rnd below, sk next st on
working rnd behind dc just made, sc in back lp of next st] 3
times, corner in next sc, join with sl st in joining sc. Fasten
off. *(40 sts)*

**Rnd 5:** With 5th colour, make slip knot on hook and join
with sc in back lp of 3rd sc of any corner, *[dc in unused
front lp of next st 1 rnd below, sk next sc on working rnd
behind dc just made, sc in back lp of next sc] 4 times,
corner in next sc; sc in back lp of next sc, rep from * twice,

**Grandma's Double Delight**
Sample project was crocheted with
Red Heart Super Saver Economy (100

[dc in unused front lp of next st 1 rnd below, sk next sc on working rnd behind dc just made, sc in back lp of next sc] 4 times, corner in next sc, join with sl st in joining sc. Fasten off. *(48 sts)*

**Rnd 6:** With A, make slip knot on hook and join with sc in back lp of 3rd sc of any corner, *[dc in unused front lp of next st 1 rnd below, sk next sc on working rnd behind dc just made, sc in back lp of next sc] 5 times, corner in next sc, sc in back lp of next sc, rep from * twice, [dc in unused front lp of next st 1 rnd below, sk next sc on working rnd behind dc just made, sc in back lp of next sc] 5 times, corner in next sc, join in joining sc. *(56 sts)*

**Rnd 7:** Ch 1, hdc in same sc as joining, *sc in next 9 sts, hdc in next 2 sts, 3 dc in centre sc of corner**, hdc in next 2 sts, rep from * twice, ending at ** on last rep, hdc in last st, join with sl st in first hdc. *(64 sts)*

Fasten off and weave in all ends.

## Assembly

Following Assembly Diagram for colour placement, join Motifs in 7 rows of 6 Motifs each. To join Motifs, hold 2 Motifs with WS tog; with tapestry needle and A, and working in back lps only, sew Motifs tog, beg and ending in 2nd dc of corners. Secure corners by working in both lps of each corner st.

## Edging

**Rnd 1 (RS):** Holding piece with RS facing and 1 short end at top, with A make slip knot on hook and join with sc in 3rd dc of upper right-hand corner, sc in next 14 sts, *hdc dec *(see Stitch Guide on page 126)* in next 2 joined dc, sc in next 15 sts, rep from * to 2nd dc on next outer corner, 3 sc in 2nd dc—*corner made*, sc in next 15 sts, **hdc dec in next 2 joined dc, sc in next 15 sts, rep from ** to 2nd dc on next

outer corner, 3 sc in 2nd dc—*corner made*, sc in next 15 sts, ***hdc dec in next 2 joined dc, sc in next 15 sts, rep from *** to 2nd dc on next outer corner, 3 sc in 2nd dc—*corner made*, sc in next 15 sts, ****hdc dec in next 2 joined dc, sc in next 15 sts, rep from **** to 2nd dc on next outer corner, 3 sc in 2nd dc—*corner made*, join with sl st in first hdc. Fasten off.

**Rnd 2:** With B, make slip knot on hook and join with sc in 2nd sc of any corner, 2 sc in same sc, *working in back lps only, sc in each sc to 2nd sc of next corner, working through both lps of sc, corner in 2nd sc, rep from * twice, working in back lps only, sc in each sc to first sc, join with sl st in joining sc. Fasten off.

**Rnd 3:** With C, make slip knot on hook and join with sc in back lp of 3rd sc of any corner, *dc in unused front lp of next sc 1 rnd below, sk next sc on working rnd behind dc just made, sc in back lp of next sc, rep from * to 2nd sc of next corner, working through both lps of sc, corner in 2nd sc; sc in back lp of next sc, **dc in unused front lp of next sc 1 rnd below, sk next sc on working rnd behind dc just made, sc in back lp of next sc, rep from ** to 2nd sc of next corner, working through both lps of sc, corner in 2nd sc; sc in back lp of next sc, ***dc in unused front lp of next sc 1 rnd below, sk next sc on working rnd behind dc just made, sc in back lp of next sc, rep from *** to 2nd sc of next corner, working through both lps of sc, corner in 2nd sc, sc in back lp of next sc, ****dc in unused front lp of next sc 1 rnd below, sk next sc on working rnd behind dc just made, sc in back lp of next sc, rep from **** to 2nd sc of next corner, working through both lps of sc, corner in 2nd sc, join with sl st in joining sc. Fasten off.

**Rnd 4:** With D, rep rnd 3.

**Rnd 5:** With E, rep rnd 3.

**Rnd 6:** With A, rep rnd 3. At end of rnd, do not fasten off.

**Rnd 7:** Ch 1, hdc in same sc as joining, *sc in each st to last 2 sts before 2nd sc of next corner, hdc in next 2 sts, 3 dc in 2nd sc of corner, hdc in next 2 sts, rep from * twice, sc in each st to last 2 sts before 2nd sc of next corner, hdc in next 2 sts, 3 dc in 2nd sc of corner, hdc in next st, join in first hdc.

Fasten off and weave in all ends. ■

| A | B | C | D | E | F |
|---|---|---|---|---|---|
| B | C | D | E | F | A |
| C | D | E | F | A | B |
| D | E | F | A | B | C |
| E | F | A | B | C | D |
| F | A | B | C | D | E |
| A | B | C | D | E | F |

**Grandma's Double Delight**
Assembly Diagram

| Motif | Rnd 1 | Rnd 2 | Rnd 3 | Rnd 4 | Rnd 5 | Rnds 6 & 7 |
|---|---|---|---|---|---|---|
| A | white | yellow | pink | blue | green | white |
| B | white | green | yellow | blue | pink | white |
| C | white | pink | blue | green | yellow | white |
| D | white | yellow | green | pink | blue | white |
| E | white | blue | pink | yellow | green | white |
| F | white | green | blue | pink | yellow | white |

**Grandma's Double Delight**
Motif Chart

# SUNSHINE AFGHAN

*Bring a little sunshine into your nursery with this easy-to-stitch afghan.*

Design | Christine Grazioso-Moody

## Skill Level
EASY

## Finished Size
47 x 47 inches

## Materials
Worsted weight yarn (1,020 yds/448g per ball):
  1 ball each pastel blue and pastel yellow
Size N/13/9mm crochet hook or size needed
  to obtain gauge
Tapestry needle

## Gauge
**With 2 strands of yarn held tog:** 4 V-sts = 4¾ inches;
  5 rows = 4¾ inches
Take time to check gauge.

## Notes
Weave in ends as work progresses.

Join with slip stitch as indicated unless otherwise stated.

Chain-3 at beginning of row counts as first double crochet unless otherwise stated.

Chain-5 at beginning of round counts as first double crochet and chain-2 space unless otherwise stated.

## Special Stitch
**V-stitch (V-st):** 2 dc in indicated place.

## Afghan
**Row 1 (RS):** With 2 strands of blue, ch 76, **V-st** *(see Special Stitch)* in 5th ch from hook, sk next ch, [V-st in next ch, sk next ch] 3 times, *drop 1 strand of blue, pick up 1 strand of yellow, [V-st in next ch, sk next ch] 4 times, drop yellow, pick up new strand of blue, [V-st in next ch, sk next ch] 4 times, rep from * 3 times, dc in last ch, turn.

**Row 2:** Ch 3 *(see Notes)*, [V-st in sp between 2 dc of next V-st] 4 times, *drop 1 strand of blue, pick up 1 strand of yellow, [V-st in sp between 2 dc of next V-st] 4 times, drop yellow, pick up 2nd strand of blue, [V-st in sp between 2 dc of next V-st] 4 times, rep from * 3 times, dc in last dc, turn.

**Rows 3 & 4:** Rep row 2.

**Row 5:** Ch 3, [V-st in sp between 2 dc of next V-st] 4 times, *drop 1 strand of blue, pick up 1 strand of yellow, [V-st in sp between 2 dc of next V-st] 4 times, drop yellow, pick up 2nd strand of blue, [V-st in sp between 2 dc of next V-st] 4 times, rep from * 3 times, dc in last dc, fasten off 1 strand of blue, pick up 1 strand of yellow, turn.

**Row 6:** Ch 3, [V-st in sp between 2 dc of next V-st] 4 times, *drop 1 strand of blue, pick up 1 strand of yellow, [V-st in sp between 2 dc of next V-st] 4 times, drop yellow, pick up 2nd strand of blue, [V-st in sp between 2 dc of next V-st] 4 times, rep from * 3 times, dc in last dc, turn.

**Rows 7–9:** Rep row 6.

Sunshine Afghan
Sample project was crocheted with Pound of Love (100 per cent acrylic) from Lion Brand.

**Row 10:** Ch 3, [V-st in sp between 2 dc of next V-st] 4 times, *drop 1 strand of blue, pick up 1 strand of yellow, [V-st in sp between 2 dc of next V-st] 4 times, drop yellow, pick up 2nd strand of blue, [V-st in sp between 2 dc of next V-st] 4 times, rep from * 3 times, dc in last dc. Fasten off yellow, pick up 1 strand of blue, turn.

**Row 11:** Ch 3, [V-st in sp between 2 dc of next V-st] 4 times, *drop 1 strand of blue, pick up 1 strand of yellow, [V-st in sp between 2 dc of next V-st] 4 times, drop yellow, pick up 2nd strand of blue, [V-st in sp between 2 dc of next V-st] 4 times, rep from * 3 times, dc in last dc, turn.

**Rows 12–41:** [Rep rows 2 to 11 consecutively] 3 times.

**Rows 42–45:** Rep rows 2 to 5. At end of last row, fasten off both colours.

## Border

**Rnd 1 (RS): Join** *(see Notes on page 92)* 2 strands of yellow in last st of row 45, **ch 5** *(see Notes on page 92)*, dc in same st *(beg corner)*, working across side, 2 dc in end of each row across, working across next side in unused lps of starting ch, (dc, ch 2, dc) in first lp *(corner)*, dc in each unused lp across to last lp, (dc, ch 2, dc) in last lp *(corner)*, working across next side in ends of rows, 2 dc in each row across, working across row 45, (dc, ch 2, dc) in first st *(corner)*, dc in each st across to beg ch-5, join in 3rd ch of beg ch-5. Fasten off.

**Rnd 2:** Join 2 strands of blue in any corner ch-2 sp, ch 1, 4 sc in same sp *(corner)*, *sc in each dc across to next corner ch-2 sp, 4 sc in corner ch-2 sp *(corner)*, rep from * twice, sc in each dc across to beg sc, join in beg sc. Fasten off. ■

# RECEIVING BLANKET & BOOTIES

*This receiving blanket and booties make a great gift for boy or girl.*

Design | Sue Childress

## Skill Level
**INTERMEDIATE**

## Booties

### Finished Size
Booties: 3½-inch sole
Blanket: 27 inches square

### Materials
Sport weight yarn (279 yds/85g per ball):
    1 ball yellow
Size F/5/3.75mm crochet hook or size needed
    to obtain gauge
1 yd ⅜-inch-wide ribbon

### Gauge
**With 2 strands of yarn held tog:** 4 V-sts = 4¾ inches;
    5 rows = 4¾ inches
Take time to check gauge.

### Notes
Chain-2 at beginning of row or round counts as first half double crochet unless otherwise stated.

Chain-3 at beginning of row or round counts as first double crochet unless otherwise stated.

Join with slip stitch as indicated unless otherwise stated.

### Bootie
Make 2

**Rnd 1:** Ch 11, 2 hdc in 3rd ch from hook *(first 2 chs count as first hdc)*, hdc in each of next 7 chs, 3 dc in last ch, working on opposite side of ch, hdc in each of next 8 chs, **join** *(see Notes)* in 2nd ch of beg ch-2. *(21 sts)*

**Rnd 2:** Ch 2 *(see Notes)*, 2 hdc in each of next 2 sts, sc in each of next 6 sts, 2 hdc in next st, 2 dc in each of next 2 sts, 2 hdc in next st, sc in each of last 8 sts, 2 hdc in same st as beg ch-2, join in 2nd ch of beg ch-2. *(29 sts)*

**Rnd 3:** Ch 2, 2 hdc in next st, hdc in each of next 3 sts, sc in each of next 7 sts, hdc in next st, (hdc, dc) in next st, 2 dc in each of next 3 sts, (dc, hdc) in next st, sc in each of next 9 sts, 2 hdc in next st, hdc in last st, join in 2nd ch of beg ch-2. *(36 sts)*

**Rnd 4:** Ch 2, **bphdc** *(see Stitch Guide on page 126)* around each st around, join in 2nd ch of beg ch-2.

**Rnd 5:** Ch 2, hdc in each of next 14 sts, [**dc dec** *(see Stitch Guide on page 126)* in next 2 sts] 3 times, hdc in each rem st around, join in 2nd ch of beg ch-2. *(33 sts)*

**Rnd 6:** Ch 2, hdc in each of next 12 sts, [dc dec in next 2 sts] 3 times, hdc in each rem st around, join in 2nd ch of beg ch-2. *(30 sts)*

**Rnd 7:** Ch 2, **hdc dec** *(see Stitch Guide on page 126)* in next 2 sts, hdc in each of next 9 sts, [dc dec in next 2 sts] twice, hdc in each rem st around, join in 2nd ch of beg ch-2. *(27 sts)*

**Rnd 8 (eyelet):** Ch 4 *(counts as first dc and ch-1)*, sk next st, dc in next st, [ch 1, sk next st, dc in next st] around, ch 1, join in 3rd ch of beg ch-4. *(14 ch sps)*

**Rnd 9:** Ch 3 *(see Notes on page 95)*, 2 dc in same ch sp, sc in next ch sp, [3 dc in next ch sp, sc in next ch sp] around, join in 3rd ch of beg ch-3. Fasten off.

Weave 18-inch piece of ribbon through ch sps on rnd 8, beg and ending in front.

# Receiving Blanket

## Materials
DK weight yarn (346 yds/100g per ball):
   2 balls yellow variegated
Size F/5/3.75mm crochet hook or size needed
   to obtain gauge

## Gauge
4 dc = 1 inch; 3 dc rows = 1¾ inches

## Note
Chain-3 at beginning of row or round counts as first double crochet unless otherwise stated.

## Special Stitch
**Cluster (cl):** Holding back last lp of each st on hook, 3 dc in place indicated, yo, pull through all sts on hook.

## Blanket

**Row 1:** Ch 104, dc in 4th ch from hook, [**dc dec** *(see Stitch Guide on page 126)* in next 2 chs] twice, *[ch 1, **cl** *(see Special Stitch)* in next ch] 5 times, ch 1**, [dc dec in next 2 sts] 6 times, rep from * across to last 6 sts, ending last rep at **, [dc dec in next 2 chs] 3 times, turn.

**Row 2:** Ch 3 *(see Note)*, dc in same st, dc in each st and in each ch across, leaving turning ch unworked, turn. *(102 dc)*

**Row 3:** Ch 3, dc in next st, [dc dec in next 2 sts] twice, *[ch 1, cl in next st] 5 times, ch 1**, [dc dec in next 2 sts] 6 times, rep from * across to last 6 sts, ending last rep at **, [dc dec in next 2 sts] 3 times, turn.

**Next rows:** [Rep rows 2 and 3 alternately] 22 times or until piece measures 27 inches. At end of last row, **do not turn.**

## Edging
Working around outer edge, ch 1, 3 hdc in end of first row, [2 hdc in end of next row, 3 hdc in end of next row] across, working in starting ch on opposite side of row 1, 3 sc in first ch, sc in each ch across with 3 sc in last ch, 3 hdc in end of first row, [2 hdc in end of next row, 3 hdc in end of next row] across, 3 sc in first st, sc in each st and ch across with 3 sc in last st, join with sl st in beg hdc. Fasten off. ∎

### Receiving Blanket & Booties

Bootie sample project was crocheted with Red Heart Designer Sport (100 per cent acrylic) from Coats & Clark.

Blanket sample project was crocheted with Baby Jacquards (90 per cent acrylic, 10 per cent nylon) from Bernat.

# FANCY FOOTWEAR

*Your baby will be steppin' out in style with a different pair of booties for every occasion.*

Design | Sheila Leslie

**Skill Level**
**EASY**

**Finished Size**
Approximately 4 inches from heel to toe

## Daisy Booties

**Materials**
DK weight yarn (395 yds/140 g per ball):
  8 yds yellow *(A)*, 8 yds white *(B)*,
  8 yds mint *(C)*
Size F/5/3.75mm crochet hook or size needed
  to obtain gauge
Tapestry needle
Stitch markers

**Gauge**
5 sc = 1 inch
Take time to check gauge.

**Special Stitch**
**Front post double crochet (fpdc):** Yo, insert hook from front to back to front around **post** *(see Stitch Guide on page 126)* of st indicated, draw lp through, [yo, draw through 2 lps on hook] twice.

**Bootie**
Make 2

**Sole**
*Note: Sole is worked in continuous rnds. Do not join unless specified, mark beg of rnds.*

**Rnd 1 (RS):** With B, ch 14, sc in 2nd ch from hook and in next 7 chs, hdc in next 4 chs, 5 hdc in last ch, working on opposite side in unused lps of beg ch, hdc in next 5 lps, sc in next 7 lps, 3 sc in last lp. *(32 sts)*

**Rnd 2:** 2 sc in next sc, sc in next 8 sts, hdc in next 5 sts, 2 hdc in each of next 3 sts, hdc in next 5 sts, sc in next 8 sts, 2 sc in each of next 2 sts. *(38 sts)*

**Rnd 3:** 2 sc in next sc, sc in next 10 sts, hdc in next 5 sts, [2 hdc in next st, hdc in next st] 3 times; hdc in next 5 sts, sc in next 7 sts, [2 sc in next st, sc in next st] twice. *(44 sts)*

**Rnd 4:** 2 sc in first sc, sc in next 15 sts, [2 sc in next st, sc in next st] 4 times, sc in next 15 sts, 2 sc in next st, sc in next 4 sts, join with sl st in first sc. *(50 sc)*

Fasten off and weave in ends.

## Instep

**Row 1 (RS):** With C, ch 8, sc in 2nd ch from hook and in each rem ch, turn. *(7 sc)*

**Row 2:** Ch 1, sc in each sc, turn.

**Rows 3–8:** Rep row 2.

**Row 9:** Ch 1, **sc dec** *(see Stitch Guide on page 126)* in first 2 sc, sc in next 3 sc, sc dec in last 2 sc. *(5 sc)*

Fasten off and weave in ends.

## Sides

*Note: Sides are worked in continuous rnds. Do not join unless specified, mark beg of rnds.*

**Rnd 1 (RS):** With A, make slip knot on hook and join with sc in side of row 1 of Instep, working in ends of rows, work 8 sc across side of Instep, working across last row of Instep, 2 sc in first sc, sc in next 3 sc, 2 sc in last sc, working across next side of Instep, work 9 sc across side, ch 25.

**Rnd 2:** Working in **back lps** *(see Stitch Guide on page 126)* only, sc in next 25 sc, sc in next 25 chs. *(50 sc)*

**Rnd 3:** Sc in each sc.

**Rnds 4 & 5:** Rep rnd 3.

Fasten off and weave in ends.

## Assembly

Holding WS of Sole facing WS of Sides, carefully matching sts, with A and beg at heel end, sl st Sole and Sides tog in back lps only of corresponding sts.

## Sock

**Rnd 1 (RS):** Starting at heel end and working in unused lps of beg ch of Sides, with B make slip knot on hook and join with sc in 13th lp before Instep, sc in next 11 lps, sc dec in next lp and first unused lp of beg ch of Instep, sc in next 5 lps, sc dec in last lp of Instep and in next unused lp of beg ch-25 of Sides, sc in next 11 lps. *(30 sc)*

**Rnd 2:** Sc in next 11 sc, sc dec, sc in next 5 sc, sc dec, sc in next 10 sc. *(28 sc)*

**Rnd 3:** Sl st in next sc, ch 3 *(counts as a dc)*, dc in each sc, join in 3rd ch of beg ch-3, change to A by drawing lp through, drop B to WS.

**Rnd 4:** Ch 1, **fpdc** *(see Special Stitch on page 98)* around beg ch-3 and around each rem dc, insert hook in first fpdc, change to B by drawing lp through st and lp on hook, drop A to WS.

**Rnd 5:** Ch 1, fpdc around each st; insert hook in first fpdc, change to A by drawing lp through st and lp on hook, drop B to WS.

**Rnd 6:** Ch 1, fpdc around each st, insert hook in first fpdc, change to B by drawing lp through st and lp on hook, drop A to WS.

**Rnds 7 & 8:** Rep rnds 5 and 6.

**Rnd 9:** Ch 1, fpdc around each st, join with sl st in first fpdc.

Fasten off and weave in all ends.

## Daisy
**Make 2**

**Rnd 1 (RS):** Starting at centre with A, ch 2, 4 sc in 2nd ch from hook. Do not join. *(4 sc)*

**Rnd 2:** 2 sc in each sc, join with sl st in first sc. *(8 sc)*

Fasten off.

**Rnd 3:** Working in **front lps** *(see Stitch Guide on page 126)* only, join B with sl st in any sc, ch 2, in same sc work (hdc, ch 2, sl st)—*beg petal made,* in each rem sc work (sl st, ch 2, hdc, ch 2, sl st)—*petal made. (8 petals)*

**Rnd 4:** Working behind petals in unused lps of rnd 2, in first lp work (sl st, ch 3, dc, ch 3, sl st), in each rem unused lp work (sl st, ch 3, dc, ch 3, sl st).

Fasten off and weave in all ends.

## Finishing
With tapestry needle and B, tack 1 Daisy to Instep of each Bootie.

# Rose Baby Booties

## Materials
DK weight yarn (395 yds/140 g per ball):
    8 yds pink (A), 8 yds white (B),
    8 yds baby pink marl (C)
Size F/5/3.75mm crochet hook or size needed
    to obtain gauge
Tapestry needle
Stitch markers

## Gauge
5 sc = 1 inch
Take time to check gauge.

## Special Stitch
**Front post double crochet (fpdc):** Yo, insert hook from front to back to front around **post** *(see Stitch Guide on page 126)* of st indicated, draw lp through, [yo, draw through 2 lps on hook] twice.

## Bootie
**Make 2**

## Sole
*Note: Sole is worked in continuous rnds. Do not join unless specified, mark beg of rnds.*

**Rnd 1 (RS):** With B, ch 14, sc in 2nd ch from hook and in next 7 chs, hdc in next 4 chs, 5 hdc in last ch, working on opposite side in unused lps of beg ch, hdc in next 5 lps, sc in next 7 lps, 3 sc in last lp. *(32 sts)*

**Rnd 2:** 2 sc in next sc, sc in next 8 sts, hdc in next 5 sts, 2 hdc in each of next 3 sts, hdc in next 5 sts, sc in next 8 sts, 2 sc in each of next 2 sts. *(38 sts)*

**Rnd 3:** 2 sc in next sc, sc in next 10 sts, hdc in next 5 sts, [2 hdc in next st, hdc in next st] 3 times, hdc in next 5 sts, sc in next 7 sts, [2 sc in next st, sc in next st] twice. *(44 sts)*

**Rnd 4:** 2 sc in first sc, sc in next 15 sts, [2 sc in next st, sc in next st] 4 times, sc in next 11 sts, 2 sc in next st, sc in next 4 sts, join with sl st in first sc. *(50 sc)*

Fasten off and weave in ends.

## Instep

**Row 1 (RS):** With A, ch 8, sc in 2nd ch from hook and in each rem ch, turn. *(7 sc)*

**Row 2:** Ch 1, sc in each sc, turn

**Rows 3–8:** Rep row 2.

**Row 9:** Ch 1, **sc dec** *(see Stitch Guide on page 126)* in first 2 sc, sc in next 3 sc, sc dec in last 2 sc. *(5 sc)*

Fasten off and weave in ends.

## Sides

*Note: Sides are worked in continuous rnds. Do not join unless specified, mark beg of rnds.*

**Rnd 1 (RS):** With A, make slip knot on hook and join with sc in side of row 1 of Instep, working in ends of rows, work 8 sc across side of Instep, working across last row of Instep, 2 sc in first sc; sc in next 3 sc, 2 sc in last sc, working across next side of Instep, work 9 sc across side, ch 25.

**Rnd 2:** Working in **back lps** *(see Stitch Guide on page 126)* only, sc in next 25 sc, sc in next 25 chs. *(50 sc)*

**Rnd 3:** Sc in each sc.

**Rnds 4 & 5:** Rep rnd 3.

Fasten off and weave in ends.

## Assembly

Holding WS of Sole facing WS of Sides, carefully matching sts, with A and beg at heel end, sl st Sole and Sides tog in back lps only of corresponding sts.

## Sock

**Rnd 1 (RS):** Starting at heel end and working in unused lps of beg ch of Sides, with B, make slip knot on hook and join with sc in 13th lp before Instep, sc in next 11 lps, sc dec in next lp and first unused lp of beg ch of Instep, sc in next 5 lps, sc dec in last lp of Instep and in next unused lp of beg ch-25 of Sides, sc in next 11 lps. *(30 sc)*

**Rnd 2:** Sc in next 11 sc, sc dec, sc in next 5 sc, sc dec, sc in next 10 sc. *(28 sc)*

**Rnd 3:** Sl st in next sc, ch 3 *(counts as a dc)*, dc in each sc, join in 3rd ch of beg ch-3, change to A by drawing lp through, drop B to WS.

**Rnd 4:** Ch 1, **fpdc** *(see Special Stitch on page 101)* around beg ch-3 and around each rem dc, insert hook in first fpdc, change to B by drawing lp through st and lp on hook, drop A to WS.

**Rnd 5:** Ch 1, fpdc around each st; insert hook in first fpdc, change to A by drawing lp through st and lp on hook, drop B to WS.

**Rnd 6:** Ch 1, fpdc around each st, insert hook in first fpdc, change to B by drawing lp through st and lp on hook, drop A to WS.

**Rnds 7 & 8:** Rep rnds 5 and 6.

**Rnd 9:** Ch 1, fpdc around each st, join with sl st in first fpdc.

Fasten off and weave in all ends.

## Rose
**Make 2**

**Rnd 1:** With C, ch 2, 6 sc in 2nd ch from hook, join with sl st in **front lp** *(see Stitch Guide on page 126)* of first sc.

**Rnd 2:** Ch 1, in same lp as joining work (sc, hdc, dc, hdc, sc, sl st)—*beg petal made,* in working in front lps only, in each rem sc work (sl st, sc, hdc, dc, hdc, sc, sl st)—*petal made. (6 petals)*

**Rnd 3:** Working behind petals in unused lps of rnd 1, [sl st in next lp, ch 3] 6 times, join with sl st in first sl st. *(6 ch-3 sps)*

**Rnd 4:** Sl st in next ch-3 sp, ch 1, in same sp and in each rem ch-3 sp work (sc, hdc, 2 dc, hdc, sc), join in first sc.

Fasten off and weave in ends.

## Finishing
With tapestry needle and C, tack 1 Rose to Instep of each Bootie.

# Mary Jane Booties

## Materials
DK weight yarn (395 yds/140 g per ball):
   8 yds soft lilac *(A)*, 8 yds white *(B)*
Sizes B/1/2.25 and F/5/3.75mm crochet hooks or size needed to obtain gauge
Tapestry needle
Stitch marker

## Gauge
**Size F hook:** 5 sc = 1 inch
Take time to check gauge.

## Special Stitch
**Front post double crochet (fpdc):** Yo, insert hook from front to back to front around **post** *(see Stitch Guide on page 126)* of st indicated, draw lp through, [yo, draw through 2 lps on hook] twice.

## Bootie
**Make 2**

## Sole
*Note: Sole is worked in continuous rnds. Do not join unless specified, mark beg of rnds.*

**Rnd 1 (RS):** With size F hook and B, ch 14, sc in 2nd ch from hook and in next 7 chs, hdc in next 4 chs, 5 hdc in last ch, working on opposite side in unused lps of beg ch, hdc in next 5 lps, sc in next 7 lps, 3 sc in last lp. *(32 sts)*

**Rnd 2:** 2 sc in next sc, sc in next 8 sts, hdc in next 5 sts, 2 hdc in each of next 3 sts, hdc in next 5 sts, sc in next 8 sts, 2 sc in each of next 2 sts. *(38 sts)*

**Rnd 3:** 2 sc in next sc, sc in next 10 sts, hdc in next 5 sts, [2 hdc in next st, hdc in next st] 3 times, hdc in next 5 sts, sc in next 7 sts, [2 sc in next st, sc in next st] twice. *(44 sts)*

**Rnd 4:** 2 sc in first sc, sc in next 15 sts, [2 sc in next st, sc in next st] 4 times, sc in next 11 sts, 2 sc in next st, sc in next 4 sts, join with sl st in first sc. *(50 sc)*

Fasten off and weave in ends.

## Instep

**Row 1 (RS):** With size F hook and B, ch 8, sc in 2nd ch from hook and in each rem ch, turn. *(7 sc)*

**Row 2:** Ch 1, sc in each sc, turn.

**Rows 3–5:** Rep row 2.

Fasten off.

**Row 6:** Holding piece with RS facing you, with A, make slip knot on hook and join with sc in first sc, sc in each rem sc, turn.

**Rows 7–8:** Rep row 2.

**Row 9:** Ch 1, **sc dec** *(see Stitch Guide on page 126)* in first 2 sc, sc in next 3 sc, sc dec in last 2 sc. *(5 sc)*

Fasten off and weave in ends.

## Sides

*Note: Sides are worked in continuous rnds. Do not join unless specified, mark beg of rnds.*

**Rnd 1 (RS):** With A make slip knot on hook and join with sc in side of row 1 of Instep, working in ends of rows, work 8 sc across side of Instep, working across last row of Instep, 2 sc in first sc; sc in next 3 sc, 2 sc in last sc; working across next side of Instep, work 9 sc across side; ch 25.

**Rnd 2:** Working in **back lps** *(see Stitch Guide on page 126)* only, sc in next 25 sc, sc in next 25 chs. *(50 sc)*

**Rnd 3:** Sc in each sc.

**Rnds 4 & 5:** Rep rnd 3.

Fasten off and weave in ends.

## Assembly
Holding WS of Sole facing WS of Sides, carefully matching sts, with A and beg at heel end, sl st Sole and Sides tog in back lps only of corresponding sts.

## Sock
**Rnd 1 (RS):** Starting at heel end and working in unused lps of beg ch of Sides, with B, make slip knot on hook and join with sc in 13th lp before Instep, sc in next 11 lps, sc dec in next lp and first unused lp of beg ch of Instep, sc in next 5 lps, sc dec in last lp of Instep and in next unused lp of beg ch-25 of Sides, sc in next 11 lps. *(30 sc)*

**Rnd 2:** Sc in next 11 sc, sc dec, sc in next 5 sc, sc dec, sc in next 10 sc. *(28 sc)*

**Rnd 3:** Sl st in back lp of next sc, ch 3 *(counts as a dc)*, working in back lps only, dc in each sc, join in 3rd ch of beg ch-3.

**Rnd 4:** Ch 1, **fpdc** *(see Special Stitch on page 103)* around beg ch-3 and around each rem dc, join with sl st in first fpdc.

**Rnd 5:** Ch 1, fpdc around each st, join with sl st in first fpdc.

**Rnds 6–9:** Rep rnd 5.

Fasten off and weave in ends.

## Ruffle

Hold piece with RS facing you and rnd 9 at bottom; starting at centre back in unused lps of rnd 2, join B in first unused lp, ch 3, *sl st in next lp, ch 3, rep from * around, join with sl st in joining sl st.

Fasten off and weave in all ends.

## Strap

Join A with sl st in first unused lp of rnd 2 at 1 side of Bootie, ch 10, sl st in corresponding unused lp on opposite side of Bootie, ch 4, sl st in same lp as last sl st made, working across strap, sl st in next 10 chs and in same lp as joining sl st made. Fasten off. Rep on rem Bootie, beg and ending Strap on opposite of Bootie.

## Bow

Make 2

**Row 1:** With size B hook and A, ch 3, sc in 2nd ch from hook and in next ch, turn. *(2 sc)*

**Row 2:** Ch 1, sc in each sc, turn.

**Row 3:** Ch 1, 2 sc in each sc, turn. *(4 sc)*

**Row 4:** Ch 1, sc in each sc, sl st in same sc as last sc made. Fasten off.

**Row 5:** Holding piece with beg ch at top, with size B hook and A, make slip knot on hook and join with sc in first unused lp of beg ch, sc in next unused lp, turn. *(2 sc)*

**Rows 6–8:** Rep rows 2 to 4.

## Tie

With size B hook and A, ch 7, sl st in 2nd ch from hook and in each rem ch. Fasten off, leaving 12-inch end for sewing.

## Finishing

Wrap 1 Tie around middle of 1 Bow, sewing ends of Tie tog at back of Bow. Tack 1 Bow to first A row of each Instep.

# Running Shoes

## Materials

DK weight yarn (395 yds/140 g per ball):
  8 yds pale blue *(A)*, 8 yds white *(B)*
Sport weight yarn 240 yds/70g per skein):
  small amount blue *(C)*
Sizes E/4/3.5mm and F/5/3.75mm crochet hooks
  or size needed to obtain gauge
Tapestry needle
Stitch markers

## Gauge

**Size F hook:** 5 sc = 1 inch

Take time to check gauge.

## Special Stitch

**Front post double crochet (fpdc):** Yo, insert hook from front to back to front around **post** *(see Stitch Guide on page 126)* of st indicated, draw lp through, [yo, draw through 2 lps on hook] twice.

## Bootie

**Make 2**

## Sole

*Note: Sole is worked in continuous rnds. Do not join unless specified, mark beg of rnds.*

**Rnd 1 (RS):** With size F hook and B, ch 14, sc in 2nd ch from hook and in next 7 chs, hdc in next 4 chs, 5 hdc in last ch, working on opposite side in unused lps of beg ch, hdc in next 5 lps, sc in next 7 lps, 3 sc in last lp. *(32 sts)*

**Rnd 2:** 2 sc in next sc, sc in next 8 sts, hdc in next 5 sts, 2 hdc in each of next 3 sts, hdc in next 5 sts, sc in next 8 sts, 2 sc in each of next 2 sts. *(38 sts)*

**Rnd 3:** 2 sc in next sc, sc in next 10 sts, hdc in next 5 sts, [2 hdc in next st, hdc in next st] 3 times, hdc in next 5 sts, sc in next 7 sts, [2 sc in next st, sc in next st] twice. *(44 sts)*

**Rnd 4:** 2 sc in first sc, sc in next 15 sts, [2 sc in next st, sc in next st] 4 times, sc in next 11 sts, 2 sc in next st, sc in next 4 sts, join with sl st in first sc. *(50 sc)*

Fasten off and weave in ends.

## Instep

**Row 1 (RS):** With size F hook and A, ch 8, sc in 2nd ch from hook and in each rem ch, turn. *(7 sc)*

**Row 2:** Ch 1, sc in each sc, turn.

**Rows 3–8:** Rep row 2.

**Row 9:** Ch 1, **sc dec** *(see Stitch Guide on page 126)* in first 2 sc, sc in next 3 sc, sc dec in last 2 sc. *(5 sc)*

Fasten off and weave in ends.

## Sides

*Note: Sides are worked in continuous rnds. Do not join unless specified, mark beg of rnds.*

**Rnd 1 (RS):** With size F hook and A, make slip knot on hook and join with sc in side of row 1 of Instep, working in ends of rows, [sc in next 4 rows, ch 3] twice, working across last row of Instep, 2 sc in first sc, sc in next 3 sc, 2 sc in last sc, ch 3, working across next side of Instep in ends of rows, [sc in next 4 rows, ch 3] twice, sc in last sc, ch 25.

**Rnd 2:** Pushing ch-3 lps toward centre and working in **back lps** *(see Stitch Guide on page 126)* only, sc in next 25 sc, sc in next 25 chs. *(50 sc)*

**Rnd 3:** Sc in each sc.

**Rnds 4 & 5:** Rep rnd 3.

Fasten off and weave in ends.

## Assembly

Holding WS of Sole facing WS of Sides, carefully matching sts, with size F hook and C and beg at heel end, sc Sole and Sides tog in back lps only of corresponding sts.

## Sock

**Rnd 1 (RS):** Starting at heel end and working in unused lps of beg ch of Sides, with size F hook and B, make slip knot on hook and join with sc in 13th lp before Instep, sc in next 11 lps, sc dec in next lp and first unused lp of beg ch of Instep, sc in next 5 lps, sc dec in last lp of Instep and in next unused lp of beg ch-25 of Sides, sc in next 11 lps. *(30 sc)*

**Rnd 2:** Sc in next 11 sc, sc dec, sc in next 5 sc, sc dec, sc in next 10 sc. *(28 sc)*

**Rnd 3:** Sl st in next sc, ch 3 *(counts as a dc)*, dc in each sc, join with sl st in 3rd ch of beg ch-3.

**Rnd 4:** Ch 1, **fpdc** *(see Special Stitch)* around beg ch-3 and around each rem dc, join with sl st in first fpdc.

**Rnd 5:** Ch 1, fpdc around each st, insert hook in first fpdc, change to A by drawing lp through st and lp on hook, drop B to WS.

**Rnd 6:** Ch 1, fpdc around each st, insert hook in first fpdc, change to B by drawing lp through st and lp on hook, drop A to WS.

**Rnd 7:** Ch 1, fpdc around each st, insert hook in first fpdc, change to C by drawing lp through st and lp on hook, drop B to WS.

**Rnd 8:** Ch 1, fpdc around each st, insert hook in first fpdc, change to B by drawing lp through st and lp on hook, drop C to WS.

**Rnd 9:** Ch 1, fpdc around each st, join with sl st in first fpdc.

Fasten off all colours and weave in all ends.

## Trim
**Make 8**

With size E hook and C, ch 6.

Fasten off and weave in ends.

## Tie
**Make 2**

With size E hook and B, ch 115.

Fasten off and weave in ends.

## Finishing

Referring to photo for placement, sew 1 Trim to side of Bootie at lp closest to Instep, from rnd 2 of Side and angled back down to joining of Sole and Sides. Sew 2nd Trim about ½ inch from first Trim, closer to toe end. Rep on other side. Rep on other Bootie with rem 4 Trims.

Lace 1 Tie through lps made on rnd 1 of Sides on 1 Bootie. Tie in bow. Rep on other Bootie. ■

# BABY SOCKS

*Fill your little one's sock drawer with different-colour socks made for 6 to 12 months size.*

Design | Darla Sims

## Skill Level

INTERMEDIATE

## Finished Size

Instructions given fit size 6–12 months.

## Materials

Sport weight yarn (279 yds/85g per ball):
  1 ball blue, small amount white
Size E/4/3.5mm crochet hook or size needed
  to obtain gauge
Stitch marker

## Gauge

9 sc = 2 inches; 6 rnds = 1 inch
Take time to check gauge.

## Note

Join with slip stitch as indicated unless otherwise stated.

# Sock

Make 2

## Cuff

**Row 1:** With blue, ch 11, sc in 2nd ch from hook and in each ch across, turn.

**Rows 2–24:** Working in **back lps** *(see Stitch Guide on page 126)*, ch 1, sc in each st across, turn.

**Row 25:** Holding row 1 and row 24 tog, working through both thicknesses, ch 1, sl st in each st across, **do not turn or fasten off.**

## Ankle

**Rnd 1:** Working in ends of rows around 1 edge, ch 1, sc in each row around, **join** *(see Note)* in beg sc.

**Rnds 2 & 3:** Ch 1, sc in each sc around, join in beg sc. Place marker in first st. At end of last rnd, fasten off.

## Heel

**Row 1 (RS):** With RS facing, and last rnd worked at top, join with sc in 5th sc to right of marker, sc in each of next 9 sts, leaving rem sts unworked, turn. *(10 sc)*

**Rows 2–4:** Ch 1, sc in each st across, turn.

**Rows 5–6:** Ch 1, **sc dec** *(see Stitch Guide on page 126)* in first 2 sts, sc in each st across with sc dec in last 2 sts, turn. Fasten off. *(6 sc at end of last row)*

## Foot

**Rnd 1 (RS):** Join with sc in 2nd sc to right of RS of Heel, sc in next st, evenly sp 5 sc in ends of rows on Heel, sc in each of next 6 sts, evenly sp 5 sc in ends of row, sc in each of last 12 sts, **do not join.** Place marker in first st of rnd. *(30 sc)*

**Rnd 2:** Sc in next st, sc dec in next 2 sts, sc in each of next 14 sts, sc dec in next 2 sts, sc in each of last 11 sts. *(28 sc)*

**Rnd 3:** Sc in next st, sc dec in next 2 sts, sc in each of next 12 sts, sc dec in next 2 sts, sc in each of last 11 sts. *(26 sc)*

**Rnd 4:** Sc in next st, sc dec in next 2 sts, sc in each of next 10 sts, sc dec in next 2 sts, sc in each of last 11 sts. *(24 sc)*

**Rnd 5:** Sc in each st around.

**Next rnds:** Rep rnd 5 until piece measures 2 inches.

## Toe
**Rnd 1:** [Sc in each of next 2 sts, sc dec in next 2 sts] around. *(18 sc)*

**Rnd 2:** [Sc in next st, sc dec in next 2 sts] around. *(12 sc)*

**Rnd 3:** [Sc dec in next 2 sts] around. Leaving long end, fasten off.

Weave long end through top of sts on last rnd, pull to close. Secure end.

## Upper Edging
**Rnd 1:** Working in ends of rows on rem side edge of Cuff, join white with sc in any row, evenly sp 26 sc around, join in beg sc.

**Rnd 2:** Ch 1, sc in each st around, join. Fasten off. ∎

**Baby Socks**
Sample project was crocheted with Red Heart Designer Sport (100 per cent acrylic) from Coats & Clark.

# RUFFLES & ROSES

*The ruffles and roses on this hat are sure to delight your little cutie.*

Design | Darla Sims

## Skill Level

EASY

## Finished Sizes
Instructions given fit size 6 months; changes for 12 months and 24 months are in [ ].

## Materials
Worsted weight yarn: (256 yds/142g per ball):
  1 ball each white and pink
Sizes G/6/4mm and H/8/5mm crochet hooks or size
  needed to obtain gauge
Tapestry needle
1 large pink satin rose
8 small pink satin roses
Sewing needle and matching thread

## Gauge
**Size H hook:** 7 sc = 2 inches
Take time to check gauge.

## Hat
*Note: Hat is worked in continuous rnds. Do not join unless specified, mark beg of rnds.*

**Rnd 1 (RS):** With size H hook and white, ch 2, 8 sc in 2nd ch from hook.

**Rnd 2:** 2 sc in each sc. *(16 sc)*

**Rnd 3:** [Sc in next sc, 2 sc in next sc] 8 times. *(24 sc)*

**Rnd 4:** [Sc in next 2 sc, 2 sc in next sc] 8 times. *(32 sc)*

**Rnd 5:** [Sc in next 3 sc, 2 sc in next sc] 8 times. *(40 sc)*

**Rnd 6:** [Sc in next 4 sc, 2 sc in next sc] 8 times. *(48 sc)*

**Rnd 7:** [Sc in next 5 sc, 2 sc in next sc] 8 times. *(56 sc)*

### For Size 6 Months Only
Continue with For All Sizes.

### For Sizes 12 & 24 Months Only
**Rnd 8:** [Sc in next 6 sc, 2 sc in next sc] 8 times. *(64 sc)*

### For Size 12 Months Only
Continue with For All Sizes.

### For Size 24 Months Only
**Rnd 9:** [Sc in next 7 sc, 2 sc in next sc] 8 times. *(72 sc)*

Continue with For All Sizes.

### For All Sizes
**Rnd 8 [9, 10]:** Ch 1, sc in each sc.

Rep rnd 8 [9, 10] until piece measures 5½ [6, 6½] inches from centre of top. Fasten off.

## Edging

With size G hook, join white in any sc of last rnd, ch 1, sc in same sc and in each rem sc, join in first sc.

Fasten off and weave in ends.

## Ruffle

Holding piece with RS facing you and last rnd worked at top, with size H hook, join white in **front lp** *(see Stitch Guide on page 126)* of any sc.

**Rnd 1:** Ch 3 *(counts as a dc)*, 2 dc in same lp, working in front lps only, 3 dc in each rem sc, join in 3rd ch of beg ch-3. Fasten off.

**Rnd 2:** Join pink in **back lp** *(see Stitch Guide on page 126)* in same lp as joining of previous rnd, ch 4 *(counts as a tr)*, 2 tr in same lp, working in back lps only, 3 tr in each rem dc, join in 4th ch of beg ch-4.

Fasten off and weave in all ends.

## Finishing

With sewing needle and matching thread, sew large rose to top of hat and sew smaller roses evenly sp around lower hat. ■

## Ruffles & Roses

Sample project was crocheted with Red Heart Soft Baby Steps (100 per cent acrylic) from Coats & Clark.

# FISHERMAN'S HAT

*Make a fisherman of your little one with this adorable hat.*

Design | Ellen Gormley

## Skill Level

�\[EASY\]

**EASY**

## Finished Size

16½ inches in circumference

## Materials

Worsted weight yarn (80 yds/50g per ball):
2 balls tan, 1 ball blue
Size G/6/4mm crochet hook or size needed
to obtain gauge
Tapestry needle
Stitch marker

## Gauge

7 sc = 1½ inches; 2 sc rnds = 1 inch
Take time to check gauge.

## Notes

Weave in loose ends as work progresses.

Do not join rounds unless otherwise stated. Use stitch marker to mark rounds, move marker as work progresses.

## Crown

**Rnd 1:** With tan, ch 4, sl st in first ch to form a ring, ch 1, 6 sc in ring, place stitch marker. *(6 sc)*

**Rnd 2:** 2 sc in each sc around. *(12 sc)*

**Rnd 3:** [Sc in next sc, 2 sc in next sc] 6 times. *(18 sc)*

**Rnd 4:** [Sc in each of next 2 sc, 2 sc in next sc] 6 times. *(24 sc)*

**Rnd 5:** [Sc in each of next 3 sc, 2 sc in next sc] 6 times. *(30 sc)*

**Rnd 6:** [Sc in each of next 4 sc, 2 sc in next sc] 6 times. *(36 sc)*

**Rnd 7:** [Sc in each of next 5 sc, 2 sc in next sc] 6 times. *(42 sc)*

**Rnd 8:** [Sc in each of next 6 sc, 2 sc in next sc] 6 times. *(48 sc)*

**Rnd 9:** [Sc in each of next 7 sc, 2 sc in next sc] 6 times. *(54 sc)*

**Rnd 10:** [Sc in each of next 8 sc, 2 sc in next sc] 6 times. *(60 sc)*

**Rnd 11:** [Sc in each of next 9 sc, 2 sc in next sc] 6 times. *(66 sc)*

**Rnd 12:** [Sc in each of next 10 sc, 2 sc in next sc] 6 times. *(72 sc)*

**Rnd 13** Working in **back lp** *(see Stitch Guide on page 126)* of each st, sc in each st around. *(72 sc)*

**Fisherman's Hat**
Sample project was crocheted
with Handicrafter Cotton (100
per cent cotton) from Bernat.

**Rnd 14:** Sc in each sc around.

**Rnds 15–21:** Rep rnd 14.

**Rnd 22:** [Sc in each of next 9 sc, ch 1, sk next sc, sc in next sc, ch 1, sk next sc] 6 times. *(60 sc, 12 ch-1 sps)*

## Brim

**Rnd 23:** Working in **front lp** *(see Stitch Guide on page 126)* of each st, sc in each st around. *(72 sc)*

**Rnd 24:** [Sc in each of next 5 sc, 2 sc in next sc] 12 times. *(84 sc)*

**Rnd 25:** [Sc in each of next 6 sc, 2 sc in next sc] 12 times. *(96 sc)*

**Rnds 26–29:** Sc in each sc around.

**Rnd 30:** Sl st in each st around. Fasten off.

## Tie

**Row 1:** With blue, ch 115. Fasten off.

Weaving Tie through rnd 22 of Crown, [insert Tie through RS into ch-1 sp to WS under sc and out through next ch-1 sp to RS] around, knot ends of Tie loosely.

## Fly

Holding blue and tan tog, wrap around 2 fingers loosely 4 times. Cut ends. With care, remove wrap from fingers. With 5-inch length each blue and tan, pass through centre of strands, knot ends to secure. Wrap a length of blue approximately ⅜ inch below top knotted section. Cut ends at bottom edge. Fray yarn ends slightly. Secure Fly to rnd 13 of Crown. ∎

# BABY'S BONNET

*Your little darling will look as cute
as a button in this flowered bonnet
stitched in cool cotton yarn.*

Design | Lainie Hering

## Skill Level

**EASY**

## Finished Size

Instructions given fit size 0–6 months or 9–18 months, depending on size of hook used.

## Materials

Cotton DK weight yarn (108 yds/50g per ball):

1 ball each dark pink, pale green,
pale yellow and light pink
Size E/4/3.75mm crochet hook (0–6 months) or size
F/5/3.75mm crochet hook (9–18 months), or size
needed to obtain gauge
1 yard ⅜-inch-wide pink ribbon

## Gauge

**Size G hook:** 14 dc = 4 inches
**Size H hook:** 12 sc = 4 inches
Take time to check gauge.

## Special Stitch

**4-double crochet cluster (4-dc cl):** Holding back last lp of each st on hook, 4 dc in next st, yo, pull through all lps on hook.

## Bonnet

**Rnd 1:** With dark pink, ch 6, sl st in first ch to form ring, ch 3 *(counts as first dc)*, 4 dc in ring, ch 3, turn, dc in each of next 3 dc, leaving last dc unworked, turn, [5 dc in ring, ch 3, turn, dc in each of next 3 dc, ch 3, leaving last dc unworked, turn] 5 times, join with sl st in top of first petal. Fasten off. *(6 petals)*

**Rnd 2:** Join pale green with sl st in any ch-3 sp, (hdc, 3 dc, hdc) in same ch sp and in each ch-3 sp around, join with sl st in top of beg hdc. Fasten off.

**Rnd 3:** Join pale yellow with sl st in sp between hdc, ch 4 *(counts as first tr)*, 6 tr in same sp, [7 tr in sp between next 2 hdc] around, join with sl st in 4th ch of beg ch-4. Fasten off. *(42 tr)*

**Rnd 4:** Join light pink with sl st in 4th tr of any 7-tr group, ch 4 *(counts as first dc and ch-1)*, dc in same st, *dc in each of next 6 sts**, (dc, ch 1, dc) in next tr, rep from * around, ending last rep at **, join with sl st in 3rd ch of beg ch-4. Fasten off. *(48 dc, 6 ch sps)*

**Rnd 5:** Join dark pink with sl st in any ch-1 sp, ch 4, dc in same ch sp, *dc in each of next 8 sts**, (dc, ch 1, dc) in next ch sp, rep from * around, ending last rep at **, join with sl st in 3rd ch of beg ch-4. Fasten off. *(60 dc, 6 ch sps)*

**Row 6:** Now working in rows, join light pink with sc in any ch-1 sp, sc in each st and in each ch sp across, turn. *(66 sc)*

**Row 7:** Working in **front lps** *(see Stitch Guide on page 126)*, ch 3, dc in each st across, turn.

**Rows 8 & 9:** Working in both lps, ch 3, dc in each st across, turn. At end of last row, fasten off.

**Row 10:** Join pale green with sl st in first st, ch 2 *(counts as first hdc)*, hdc in each st across, turn. Fasten off.

**Row 11:** Join pale yellow with sl st in first st, ch 2, dc in next st, [**4–dc cl** *(see Special Stitch on page 115)* in next st, dc in each of next 3 sts] across, turn. Fasten off.

**Row 12:** Rep row 10.

**Row 13:** With dark pink, rep row 10.

**Row 14:** Join light pink with sl st in first st, ch 3, dc in each st across, turn.

**Row 15:** Ch 3, dc in each st across, turn.

**Rows 16 & 17:** Ch 1, sc in each st across, turn.

**Row 18:** Ch 4, tr in same st, 2 tr in each st across. Fasten off.

**Row 19:** Join pale green with sc in first st, sc in next st, (ch 1, sc) in each st across, ending with sc in last st. Fasten off.

## Ruffle

With front facing, working in rem lps on row 6, join light pink with sc in first st, sk next st, [5 dc in next st, sk next st, sc in next st, sk next st] across. Fasten off.

## Neck Trim

**Row 1:** Working in end of rows, join light pink with sc in row 17, evenly sp sc across to opposite end of row 17, turn.

**Row 2:** Ch 1, sc in each st across, turn. Fasten off.

## Tie

Weave ribbon through row 15, over 3 sts, under 1 st.

Tie knot in ribbon at each end of row 15 on inside. ■

**Baby's Bonnet**
Sample project was crocheted
with Cotton Classic (100 per cent
mercerized cotton) from Tahki.

# TEDDY BEAR SET

*This darling hat and booties set will keep baby warm from head to toe.*

Design | Nanette Seale

## Skill Level
EASY

## Finished Sizes
Hat: 12 months
Booties: Instructions given fit 5-inch sole; changes for
 5½-inch sole are in [ ].

## Materials
Worsted weight yarn (364 yds/198g per skein):
 1 skein each light blue and tan, small amount
 dark brown and black
Size G/6/4mm crochet hook or size needed
 to obtain gauge
Tapestry needle

## Gauge
15 sts = 4 inches
Take time to check gauge.

# Hat
With light blue, ch 26.

**Row 1 (WS):** Sc in 2nd ch from hook and in each rem ch, turn. *(25 sc)*

**Row 2 (RS):** Ch 1, working in **back lps** *(see Stitch Guide on page 126)* only, hdc in each sc, turn.

**Row 3:** Ch 1, working in back lps only, sc in hdc, turn.

**Rows 4–44:** Rep rows 2 and 3.

**Row 45:** Hold unused lps of beg ch behind row 44, working in back lps only of row 44 and in unused lps of beg ch at same time, sl st in each st. Do not fasten off.

## Top
Turn hat inside out. You will now be working across the ends of rows to fill in top of hat.

**Rnd 1:** Ch 1, working across long edge in ends of rows, sc in each row; join in first sc. *(44 sc)*

**Rnd 2:** Ch 1, sc in first 2 sc, *sc dec *(see Stitch Guide on page 126)* in next 2 sc, sc in next 2 sc, rep from * around, join in first sc. *(33 sc)*

**Rnd 3:** Ch 1, sc in first 2 sc, *sc dec; sc in next 2 sc, rep * to last 3 sc, sc dec, sc in last sc, join in first sc. *(25 sc)*

**Rnd 4:** Ch 1, sc in first 2 sc, *sc dec, sc in next 2 sc, rep from * to last 3 sc, sc dec, sc in last sc, join in first sc. *(19 sc)*

**Rnd 5:** Ch 1, [sc dec] 9 times, sc in last sc, join in first sc. *(10 sc)*

**Rnd 6:** Ch 1, [sc dec] 5 times, join in first sc. *(5 sc)*

Fasten off, leaving an 8-inch end.

Weave long strand through sts to close opening.

## Face
*Note: Face is worked in continuous rnds. Do not join unless specified; mark beg of rnds.*

**Teddy Bear Set**
Sample projects were crocheted
with Red Heart Economy (100 per
cent acrylic) from Coats & Clark.

Cross end of tan to form lp.

**Rnd 1 (RS):** Ch 1, 6 sc in lp, tighten lp. Do not join. *(6 sc)*

**Rnd 2:** 2 sc in each sc. *(12 sc)*

**Rnd 3:** Sc in next sc, [2 sc in next sc, sc in next sc] 6 times. *(18 sc)*

**Rnd 4:** Sc in next 2 sc, [2 sc in next sc, sc in next 2 sc] 6 times. *(24 sc)*

**Rnd 5:** Sc in next 3 sc, [2 sc in next sc, sc in next 3 sc] 6 times. *(30 sc)*

**Rnd 6:** Sc in next 4 sc, [2 sc in next sc, sc in next 4 sc] 6 times. *(36 sc)*

**Rnd 7:** Sc in next 5 sc, [2 sc in next sc, sc in next 5 sc] 6 times, join in first sc. *(42 sc)*

Fasten off, leaving an 8-inch end for sewing.

## Ear
**Make 2**

Cross end of tan to form lp, ch 3, 9 dc in lp, tighten lp, do not join. Fasten off.

## Eye
**Make 2**

Cross end of dark brown to form lp, ch 1, 6 sc in lp, tighten lp, join in first sc. Fasten off, leaving an 8-inch end for sewing.

## Nose

Cross end of dark brown to form lp, ch 1, 6 sc in lp, tighten lp, do not join. Fasten off, leaving a 8-inch end for sewing.

## Finishing

**Step 1:** With black, make small **French knot** *(see illustration)* in centre of each Eye. Referring to photo for placement, sew Eyes to Face.

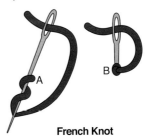

**French Knot**

**Step 2:** Flatten Nose piece so first and last sts form straight edge. Sew Nose to Face. With brown, embroider mouth using **straight sts** *(see illustration)*.

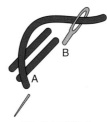

**Straight Stitch**

**Step 3:** Flatten Ear so first and last dc sts form straight edge. Sew straight edge of each Ear to top of Face, about 1 inch apart.

**Step 4:** Sew Face to top of Hat, leaving tops of Ears unsewn.

# Bootie
**Make 2**

With light blue, ch 12 [16].

**Rnd 1:** 3 hdc in 3rd ch from hook *(beg 2 sk hdc count as a hdc),* hdc in next 8 [12] chs, 6 hdc in next ch, work in unused lps on opposite side of beg ch, hdc in next 8 [12] lps, join in 2nd ch of beg 2 sk chs. *(26 [34] sc)*

**Rnd 2:** Ch 1, 2 sc in same ch as joining; [sc in next st, 2 sc in next st] twice, sc in next 7 [11] sts, 2 sc in next 6 sts, sc in next 8 [11] sts, join in first sc. *(25 [42] sc)*

**Rnd 3:** Ch 2 *(counts as a hdc on this and following rnds),* hdc in next sc, 2 hdc in next sc, hdc in next 2 sc, 2 hdc in next sc, hdc in next 11 [15] sc, [2 hdc in next sc, hdc in next 2 sc] 4 times, hdc in next 6 [9] sc, join in 2nd ch of beg ch-2. *(41 [48] hdc)*

**Rnd 4:** Ch 1, sc in each hdc, join in first sc.

**Rnd 5:** Ch 2, hdc in next sc, [hdc dec *(see Stitch Guide on page 126)* in next 2 sc, hdc in next 2 sc] twice, hdc in each rem sc, join in 2nd ch of beg ch-2. *(39 [46] hdc)*

**Rnd 6:** Ch 1, sc in same ch as joining, [sc dec, sc in next hdc] 4 times, sc in each rem hdc, join in first sc. *(35 [42] sc)*

**Rnd 7:** Ch 2, [hdc dec, hdc in next sc] 3 times, hdc in each rem sc, join in 2nd ch of beg ch-2. *(32 [39] hdc)*

**Rnd 8:** Ch 1, sc in same ch as joining, [sc dec, sc in next hdc] 3 times, sc in each hdc to last 2 hdc, sc dec, join in first sc. *(28 [35] hdc)*

**Rnd 9:** Ch 2, [hdc dec] 3 times, hdc in each sc to last 2 sc, hdc dec, join in 2nd ch of beg ch-2. *(24 [31] hdc)*

**Rnd 10:** Ch 1, sc in same ch as joining and in each rem hdc, join in first sc.

## Ribbing
Ch 8, sc in 2nd ch from hook and in each rem ch, *sl st in next 2 sc on rnd 10, ch 1, turn, sk 2 sl sts just made, working in **back lps** *(see Stitch Guide on page 126)* only, hdc in each sc, turn, ch 1, working in back lps only, sc in each hdc, rep from * around the sts of Rnd 10, end with sl st in last st of Rnd 10, turn, ch 1, sk the last sl st made, hdc in back lps of each sc across.

Fasten off.

Sew edges of the ribbing tog in back lps.

## Face
### Make 2

*Note: Face is worked in continuous rnds. Do not join unless specified, mark beg of rnds.*

Cross end of tan to form lp.

**Rnd 1:** Ch 1, 6 sc in lp, tighten lp. *(6 sc)*

**Rnd 2:** 2 sc in each sc. *(12 sc)*

**Rnd 3:** Sc in next sc, [2 sc in next sc, sc in next sc] 6 times, join in first sc. *(18 sc)*

**Rnd 4:** Ch 1, in same sc as joining work (sc, hdc), 2 hdc in next sc, in next sc work (hdc, sc), sl st in next 3 sc, in next sc work (sc, hdc), 2 hdc in next sc, in next sc work (hdc, sc), join in st.

Fasten off and weave in ends.

## Finishing
Referring to photo for placement and with dark brown, make small French knot for each eye and nose on each Face. With straight sts, embroider mouth.

Sew Faces to tops of Booties, leaving tops of ears unsewn. ■

# INDEX

Sunday Pink, 20

Baby Set, 26

Teddy & Me Bibs, 31

Beach Baby Ensemble, 36

Pretty in Pink Sweater, 43

White Ruffled Baby Dress, 46

Little Boy Blue, 50

Seaside Cardigan, 57

Baby Letter Jacket, 68

Little Mountain Man, 72

# INDEX

# GENERAL INFORMATION

## Standard Yarn Weight System
Categories of yarn, gauge ranges and recommended needle and hook sizes

| Yarn Weight Symbol & Category Names | 1 SUPER FINE | 2 FINE | 3 LIGHT | 4 MEDIUM | 5 BULKY | 6 SUPER BULKY |
|---|---|---|---|---|---|---|
| Type of Yarns in Category | Sock, Fingering, Baby | Sport, Baby | DK, Light Worsted | Worsted, Afghan, Aran | Chunky, Craft, Rug | Bulky, Roving |
| Crochet Gauge* Ranges in Single Crochet to 4 inch | 21–32 sts | 16–20 sts | 12–17 sts | 11–14 sts | 8–11 sts | 5–9 sts |
| Recommended Hook in Metric Size Range | 2.25–3.5 mm | 3.5–4.5 mm | 4.5–5.5 mm | 5.5–6.5 mm | 6.5–9 mm | 9 mm and larger |
| Recommended Hook U.S. Size Range | B1–E4 | E4–7 | 7–I–9 | I–9–K–10½ | K–10½–M–13 | M–13 and larger |

\* GUIDELINES ONLY: The above reflect the most commonly used gauges and needle sizes for specific yarn categories.

## Skill Levels

**BEGINNER**

Beginner projects for first-time crocheters using basic stitches. Minimal shaping.

**EASY**

Easy projects using basic stitches, repetitive stitch patterns, simple colour changes and simple shaping and finishing.

**INTERMEDIATE**

Intermediate projects with a variety of stitches, mid-level shaping and finishing.

**EXPERIENCED**

Experienced projects using advanced techniques and stitches, detailed shaping and refined finishing.

# Metric Conversion Charts

## METRIC CONVERSIONS

| | | | | |
|---|---|---|---|---|
| yards | x | .9144 | = | metres (m) |
| yards | x | 91.44 | = | centimetres (cm) |
| inches | x | 2.54 | = | centimetres (cm) |
| inches | x | 25.40 | = | millimetres (mm) |
| inches | x | .0254 | = | metres (m) |

| | | | | |
|---|---|---|---|---|
| centimetres | x | .3937 | = | inches |
| metres | x | 1.0936 | = | yards |

## INCHES INTO MILLIMETRES & CENTIMETRES (Rounded off slightly)

| inches | mm | cm | inches | cm | inches | cm | inches | cm |
|---|---|---|---|---|---|---|---|---|
| 1/8 | 3 | 0.3 | 5 | 12.5 | 21 | 53.5 | 38 | 96.5 |
| 1/4 | 6 | 0.6 | 5½ | 14 | 22 | 56 | 39 | 99 |
| 3/8 | 10 | 1 | 6 | 15 | 23 | 58.5 | 40 | 101.5 |
| 1/2 | 13 | 1.3 | 7 | 18 | 24 | 61 | 41 | 104 |
| 5/8 | 15 | 1.5 | 8 | 20.5 | 25 | 63.5 | 42 | 106.5 |
| 3/4 | 20 | 2 | 9 | 23 | 26 | 66 | 43 | 109 |
| 7/8 | 22 | 2.2 | 10 | 25.5 | 27 | 68.5 | 44 | 112 |
| 1 | 25 | 2.5 | 11 | 28 | 28 | 71 | 45 | 114.5 |
| 1¼ | 32 | 3.2 | 12 | 30.5 | 29 | 73.5 | 46 | 117 |
| 1½ | 38 | 3.8 | 13 | 33 | 30 | 76 | 47 | 119.5 |
| 1¾ | 45 | 4.5 | 14 | 35.5 | 31 | 79 | 48 | 122 |
| 2 | 50 | 5 | 15 | 38 | 32 | 81.5 | 49 | 124.5 |
| 2½ | 65 | 6.5 | 16 | 40.5 | 33 | 84 | 50 | 127 |
| 3 | 75 | 7.5 | 17 | 43 | 34 | 86.5 | | |
| 3½ | 90 | 9 | 18 | 46 | 35 | 89 | | |
| 4 | 100 | 10 | 19 | 48.5 | 36 | 91.5 | | |
| 4½ | 115 | 11.5 | 20 | 51 | 37 | 94 | | |

## KNITTING NEEDLES CONVERSION CHART

| U.S. | 0 | 1 | 2 | 3 | 4 | 5 | 6 | 7 | 8 | 9 | 10 | 10½ | 11 | 13 | 15 |
|---|---|---|---|---|---|---|---|---|---|---|---|---|---|---|---|
| Canada/U.K. | 14 | 13 | 12 | 10 | - | 9 | 8 | 7 | 6 | 5 | 4 | 3 | 0 | 00 | 000 |
| Metric (mm) | 2 | 2¼ | 2¾ | 3¼ | 3½ | 3¾ | 4 | 4½ | 5 | 5½ | 6 | 6½ | 8 | 9 | 10 |

## CROCHET HOOKS CONVERSION CHART

| U.S. | 1/B | 2/C | 3/D | 4/E | 5/F | 6/G | 8/H | 9/I | 10/J | 10½/K | 15/N |
|---|---|---|---|---|---|---|---|---|---|---|---|
| Canada/U.K. | 13 | - | 10 | 9 | - | 8 | 6 | 5 | 4 | 3 | 000 |
| Metric (mm) | 2.25 | 2.75 | 3.25 | 3.5 | 3.75 | 4 | 5 | 5.5 | 6 | 6.5 | 10 |

# STITCH GUIDE

**Chain (ch):** Yo, pull through lp on hook.

**Slip stitch (sl st):** Insert hook in st, pull through both lps on hook.

**Front loop (front lp) Back loop (back lp)**

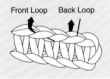

Front Loop     Back Loop

**Single crochet (sc):** Insert hook in st, yo, pull through st, yo, pull through both lps on hook.

**Front post stitch (fp): Back post stitch (bp):** When working post st, insert hook from right to left around post st on previous row.

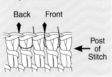

Back     Front

Post of Stitch

**Half double crochet (hdc):** Yo, insert hook in st, yo, pull through st, yo, pull through all 3 lps on hook.

**Double treble crochet (dtr):** Yo 3 times, insert hook in st, yo, pull through st, [yo, pull through 2 lps] 4 times.

**Change colours:** Drop first colour; with 2nd colour, pull through last 2 lps of st.

**Double crochet (dc):** Yo, insert hook in st, yo, pull through st, [yo, pull through 2 lps] twice.

**Treble crochet (tr):** Yo twice, insert hook in st, yo, pull through st, [yo, pull through 2 lps] 3 times.

**Single crochet decrease (sc dec):** (Insert hook, yo, draw lp through) in each of the sts indicated, yo, draw through all lps on hook.

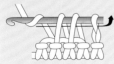

Example of 2-sc dec

**Half double crochet decrease (hdc dec):** (Yo, insert hook, yo, draw lp through) in each of the sts indicated, yo, draw through all lps on hook.

Example of 2-hdc dec

**Double crochet decrease (dc dec):** (Yo, insert hook, yo, draw loop through, draw through 2 lps on hook) in each of the sts indicated, yo, draw through all lps on hook.

Example of 2-dc dec

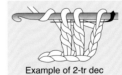

Example of 2-tr dec

**Treble crochet decrease (tr dec):** Holding back last lp of each st, tr in each of the sts indicated, yo, pull through all lps on hook.

| US | | UK |
|---|---|---|
| sl st (slip stitch) | = | sc (single crochet) |
| sc (single crochet) | = | dc (double crochet) |
| hdc (half double crochet) | = | htr (half treble crochet) |
| dc (double crochet) | = | tr (treble crochet) |
| tr (treble crochet) | = | dtr (double treble crochet) |
| dtr (double treble crochet) | = | ttr (triple treble crochet) |
| skip | = | miss |

# FEELING CRAFTY? GET CREATIVE!

Each 160-page book features easy-to-follow, step-by-step instructions and full-page colour photographs of every project. Whatever your crafting fancy, there's a Company's Coming Creative Series craft book to match!

## Beading: Beautiful Accessories in Under an Hour
Complement your wardrobe, give your home extra flair or add an extra-special personal touch to gifts with these quick and easy beading projects. Create any one of these special crafts in an hour or less.

## Knitting: Easy Fun for Everyone
Take a couple of needles and some yarn and see what beautiful things you can make! Learn how to make fashionable sweaters, comfy knitted blankets, scarves, bags and other knitted crafts with these easy-to-intermediate knitting patterns.

## Card Making: Handmade Greetings for All Occasions
Making your own cards is a fun, creative and inexpensive way of letting someone know you care. Stamp, emboss, quill or layer designs in a creative and unique card with your own personal message for friends or family.

## Patchwork Quilting
In this book full of throws, baby quilts, table toppers, wall hangings—and more—you'll find plenty of beautiful projects to try. With the modern fabrics available, and the many practical and decorative applications, patchwork quilting is not just for Grandma!

## Crocheting: Easy Blankets, Throws & Wraps
Find projects perfect for decorating your home, for looking great while staying warm or for giving that one-of-a-kind gift. A range of simple but stunning designs make crocheting quick, easy and entertaining.

## Sewing: Fun Weekend Projects
Find a wide assortment of easy and attractive projects to help you create practical storage solutions, decorations for any room or just the right gift for that someone special. Create table runners, placemats, baby quilts, pillows and more!

*For a complete listing of Company's Coming cookbooks and craft books, check out*

**www.companyscoming.com**

We have a tasty lineup of cookbooks, with plenty more in the oven.

www.companyscoming.com

- Preview new titles
- Exclusive cookbook offers
- Find titles no longer in stores

*Sign up for our FREE newsletter and receive kitchen-tested recipes every month!*

Company's Coming